EYEWITNESS
HURRICANE & TORNADO

Cyclone shelter

Spots on the Sun

Sunset at Stonehenge, England

19th-century
reproduction of
Galileo's thermoscope

Saturn

Lighthouse
at the George
Washington Bridge
in New York City

Wind-eroded
rocks in
Utah

Ice crystal

Pinecone's open scales indicate dry weather

EYEWITNESS
HURRICANE & TORNADO

Written by
JACK CHALLONER

Simultaneous waterspout and lightning bolt

Doppler-radar dome

Storm system viewed from space

Avalanche-warning sign

DK

LONDON, NEW YORK,
MELBOURNE, MUNICH, AND DELHI

Project editor Melanie Halton
Art editor Ann Cannings
Managing editor Sue Grabham
Senior managing art editor Julia Harris
Editorial consultant Lesley Newson
Picture research Mollie Gillard, Samantha Nunn
DTP designers Andrew O'Brien, Georgia Bryer
Production Kate Oliver

RELAUNCH EDITION (DK UK)
Editor Ashwin Khurana
US editor Margaret Parrish
Senior designers Rachael Grady, Spencer Holbrook
Managing editor Gareth Jones
Managing art editor Philip Letsu
Publisher Andrew Macintyre
Producer, pre-production Adam Stoneham
Senior producer Charlotte Cade
Jacket editor Manisha Majithia, Maud Whatley
Jacket designer Laura Brim
Jacket design development manager Sophia MTT
Publishing director Jonathan Metcalf
Associate publishing director Liz Wheeler
Art director Phil Ormerod

RELAUNCH EDITION (DK INDIA)
Senior editor Neha Gupta
Art editors Deep Shikha Walia, Shreya Sadhan
Senior DTP designer Harish Aggarwal
DTP designer Pawan Kumar
Managing editor Alka Thakur Hazarika
Managing art editor Romi Chakraborty
CTS manager Balwant Singh
Jacket editorial manager Saloni Talwar
Jacket designer Vidit Vashisht

First American Edition, 1995
This American Edition, 2014
Published in the United States by DK Publishing
4th floor, 345 Hudson Street
New York, New York 10014

14 15 16 17 18 10 9 8 7 6 5 4 3
002-196431-07/14

A catalog record for this book is available from the Library of Congress.

ISBN 978-1-4654-2053-4 (Paperback)
ISBN 978-1-4654-2095-4 (ALB)

DK books are available at special discounts when purchased in bulk for sales
promotions, premiums, fund-raising, or educational use. For details, contact:
DK Publishing Special Markets, 345 Hudson Street, New York, New York 10014 or
SpecialSale@dk.com.

Color reproduction by Alta Image Ltd., London, UK
Printed and bound by South China Printing Co. Ltd., China

Discover more at

www.dk.com

Venetian blind twisted by a tornado

Storm erupts on the Sun

Hurricane-warning flags

Italian thermometer (1657)

Contents

Icicle formation in Arizona

Weather folklore

In ancient times, people didn't know how the weather worked. Some realized that clouds were made of water, but they did not understand the wind or the Sun. Many believed the gods made the weather; others observed plants, animals, or the sky to deduce a forecast. Some of these observations were reliable, but an accurate forecast requires a full understanding of how the weather works. Weather science was begun by philosophers in ancient Greece, but they did not test their theories, and so they were often wrong.

Cone watch
Pinecones open their scales in dry air and close them when it is humid. Air is normally humid before rainfall, so pinecones can help forecast wet weather.

Italian fresco showing Plato and Aristotle (1511)

Thinkers
Ancient Greek philosophers Aristotle and Plato were among the first people to try to explain scientifically how the weather works, including cloud, hail, storm, and snow formation, plus Sun haloes. Their ideas were very influential and were not challenged for about 2,000 years.

Rain cry
These Yali tribesmen of New Guinea are performing a dance to call for rain. Dancers carry grass, which is believed to pierce the eye of the Sun and make it cry tears of rain.

Animal forecast
Many animals respond to changes in temperature, humidity, or atmospheric pressure, such as roosters, which often crow before a thunderstorm. Observing animals can help with weather forecasts.

Sun worship

Throughout history, many cultures have worshiped the Sun. Stonehenge in England is thought to be an ancient place of Sun worship. Some stones line up to where the Sun rises on the summer solstice (when the Sun is at its highest).

Stonehenge was built between 3000 BCE and 1500 BCE

Sky watching

An ancient Maori myth describes Tawhaki, the god of thunder and lightning, going up to the sky disguised as a kite. Maori priests believed they could predict the weather by flying kites and watching how they moved across the sky.

Maori kite made of canvas and twigs

Magic charms

This figurehead from the Solomon Islands would have been on the front of a canoe to ward off dangerous storms at sea. Many lucky charms that are used to protect people against bad weather are linked to gods or spirits.

Stormy tale

In the Shinto religion, divine being Amaterasu Omikami lights up heaven. Her brother, a storm god, causes strong winds and floods, which make Amaterasu hide in a cave and the world go dark—just like during a storm.

Statue of Chac, Mayan rain god

Weather sacrifice

Legend says that the Mayan rain god, Chac, sent rain for crops, but also storms, which destroyed crops. People made offerings to Chac to keep the rains but stop the storms.

Bushy tailed squirrel

Furry tale

Some people believe that the bushier a squirrel's tail is during fall, the harsher the winter will be. There is no scientific evidence for this.

Early forecasts

Meteorology, or modern weather science, began about 300 years ago when people started to experiment scientifically with water, heat, and air—the components of weather. They learned about atmospheric pressure, the gases of air, and water evaporation. Early meteorologists invented crude measuring devices to test theories. Important developments were the barometer (measures atmospheric pressure), the thermometer (measures temperature), and hygrometer (measures humidity). Today, sophisticated equipment allows accurate predictions of extreme weather.

Glass bulb

Under pressure

In 1643, Italian physicist Evangelista Torricelli made the first barometer—a 3-ft- (1-m-) long tube filled with mercury and put upside down in a bowl of mercury. The weight, or pressure, of air on the mercury in the bowl stopped the mercury in the tube from falling below 30 in (76 cm).

Moving mercury

Meteorologist Robert Fitzroy invented this barometer, which has a scale to measure the mercury column. Fine weather is forecast when atmospheric pressure pushes the mercury column above 30 in (76 cm); unsettled weather is predicted when it falls below this.

Fitzroy barometer

High temperature

Italian physicist Galileo Galilei designed this thermoscope (early thermometer) about 400 years ago. A long tube with a bulb at the end sat in a flask of water. As the temperature rose, air in the bulb expanded, causing the water level in the tube to drop. As it became cooler, the air contracted and the water level rose.

Flask would have been filled with water

Cotton bag for absorbing moisture in the air

Invisible water

Air normally becomes humid (contains more water) before a thunderstorm. The water in the air is an invisible vapor, but a hygrometer, designed about 350 years ago, is able to measure it. Water is absorbed from the air by the cotton bag, which becomes heavier. The greater the humidity, the more the bag drops down.

Balancing weight made of glass

A 19th-century reproduction of Galileo's original thermoscope

17th-century balance hygrometer

When the water level
in the spout is high,
air pressure is low,
and storms can
be expected

When working,
the level of
water in the
weather glass
would have been
much higher

Weather Glass

In this simple
barometer,
atmospheric
pressure
pushes down on
the water in the
sealed flask arm.
The air inside the
arm pushes in the other
direction. As atmospheric
pressure changes, the water
level rises and falls. Before a
storm, air pressure drops, and
the water rises up the arm.

Scorch marks on paper

Image of Sun
is reflected in
the glass orb

Sunshine
recorder

Focused measurement

This glass ball focuses
sunlight on paper. As the Sun
moves across the sky, the trail of
scorches shows the amount of sunlight.
If clouds hide the Sun, there is not
enough sunlight to scorch the paper.

Thick needle aligns with the normal
path of storms in the region

Thin needle indicates safe
course away from the storm

Hotness scale

When this thermometer
was made, in 1657, there
was no agreed scale for
reading measurements.
Today, meteorologists use
two main scales to record
temperature—Celsius
and Fahrenheit. Both
scales were invented in
the 18th century.

Ornate thermometer
made in Italy, 1657

An eye on the storm

Cyclonic winds spiral at their center,
and so, before hurricane radio warnings,
sailors used this barocyclonometer to
measure changes in wind direction and
atmospheric pressure. They could then
work out which way the hurricane was
moving and steer their vessels to safety.

A hotty

The spiraling
tube of this glass
thermometer
saves space. When
the temperature
increases, water
in the lower bulb
expands, filling more
of the spiral tube. The
higher the water in
the tube, the higher
the temperature.

It's a gas

During the 1770s,
French chemist
Antoine Lavoisier
was the first person
to discover that the
atmosphere is a
mixture of gases.
He also found that
hydrogen and
oxygen combine
to make water.

What is extreme weather?

From hurricanes and tornadoes, droughts and floods to freezing and high temperatures, extreme weather can be dangerous. Weather can be described by wind speed, temperature, atmospheric pressure, and precipitation (rain, hail, or snow). The average world temperature is 59°F (15°C), but some places are colder or warmer. The average rainfall is 39 in (100 cm) per year, but some places have no rain, others too much and all at once. Extreme weather can happen where weather is usually calm.

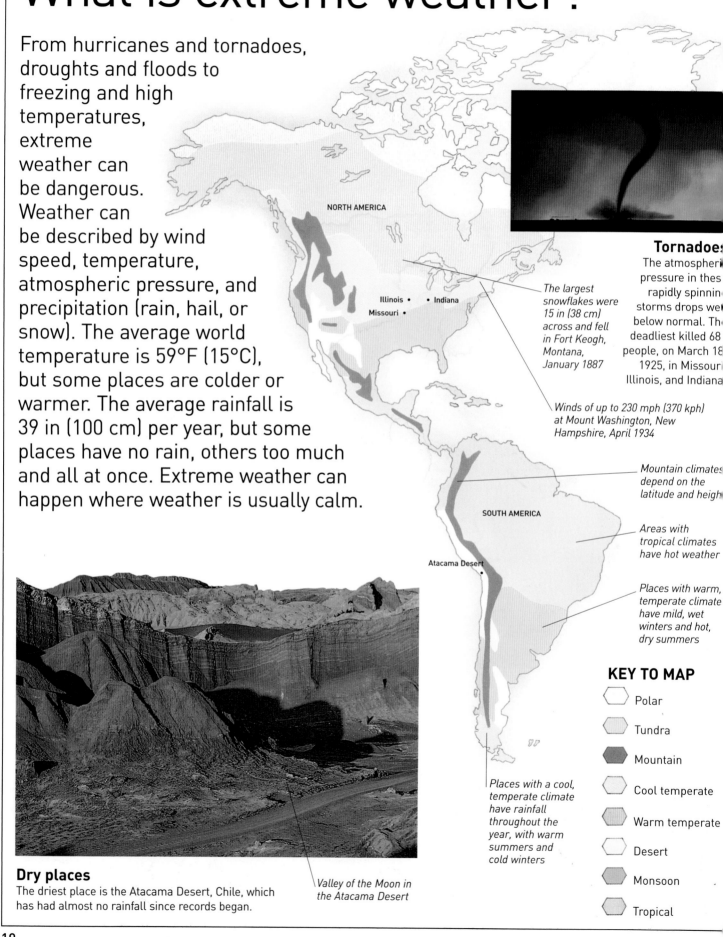

NORTH AMERICA

Illinois •   • Indiana
Missouri •

Tornadoes
The atmospheric pressure in these rapidly spinning storms drops well below normal. The deadliest killed 689 people, on March 18 1925, in Missouri, Illinois, and Indiana

The largest snowflakes were 15 in (38 cm) across and fell in Fort Keogh, Montana, January 1887

Winds of up to 230 mph (370 kph) at Mount Washington, New Hampshire, April 1934

Mountain climates depend on the latitude and height

SOUTH AMERICA

Areas with tropical climates have hot weather

Atacama Desert

Places with warm, temperate climate have mild, wet winters and hot, dry summers

KEY TO MAP

- Polar
- Tundra
- Mountain
- Cool temperate
- Warm temperate
- Desert
- Monsoon
- Tropical

Places with a cool, temperate climate have rainfall throughout the year, with warm summers and cold winters

Dry places
The driest place is the Atacama Desert, Chile, which has had almost no rainfall since records began.

Valley of the Moon in the Atacama Desert

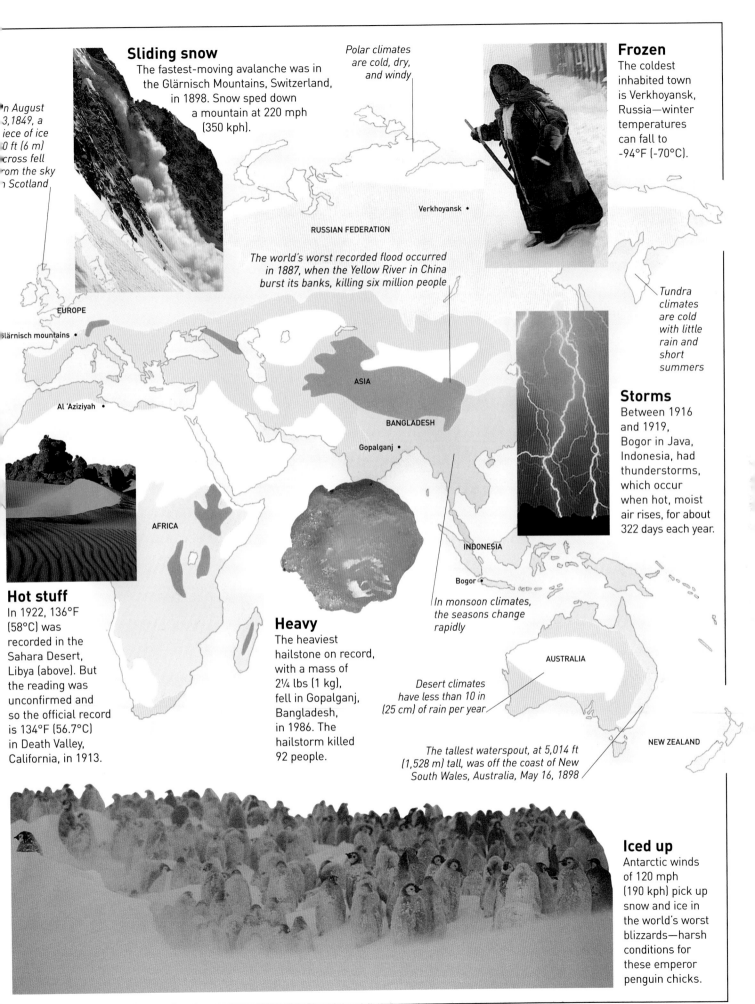

Sliding snow
The fastest-moving avalanche was in the Glärnisch Mountains, Switzerland, in 1898. Snow sped down a mountain at 220 mph (350 kph).

Polar climates are cold, dry, and windy

Frozen
The coldest inhabited town is Verkhoyansk, Russia—winter temperatures can fall to -94°F (-70°C).

In August 3,1849, a iece of ice 0 ft (6 m) cross fell rom the sky n Scotland

Verkhoyansk •

RUSSIAN FEDERATION

The world's worst recorded flood occurred in 1887, when the Yellow River in China burst its banks, killing six million people

EUROPE

Glärnisch mountains •

Tundra climates are cold with little rain and short summers

ASIA

Al 'Aziziyah •

BANGLADESH

Gopalganj •

Storms
Between 1916 and 1919, Bogor in Java, Indonesia, had thunderstorms, which occur when hot, moist air rises, for about 322 days each year.

AFRICA

INDONESIA

Bogor •

In monsoon climates, the seasons change rapidly

Hot stuff
In 1922, 136°F (58°C) was recorded in the Sahara Desert, Libya (above). But the reading was unconfirmed and so the official record is 134°F (56.7°C) in Death Valley, California, in 1913.

Heavy
The heaviest hailstone on record, with a mass of 2¼ lbs (1 kg), fell in Gopalganj, Bangladesh, in 1986. The hailstorm killed 92 people.

Desert climates have less than 10 in (25 cm) of rain per year

AUSTRALIA

NEW ZEALAND

The tallest waterspout, at 5,014 ft (1,528 m) tall, was off the coast of New South Wales, Australia, May 16, 1898

Iced up
Antarctic winds of 120 mph (190 kph) pick up snow and ice in the world's worst blizzards—harsh conditions for these emperor penguin chicks.

Extreme causes

Important factors that affect the weather include the Sun heating the Earth and differences in atmospheric pressure. Dust from volcanoes and storms on the Sun's surface can also make the weather hotter or colder, and wetter or drier. Pollution in the atmosphere also affects the weather. Causes of extreme weather are understood, but predicting weather more than a few days ahead is still impossible because the weather is a complex and sensitive system.

Chaotic weather
According to the chaos theory—the study of unpredictable systems— a butterfly can change the course of the weather; weather is so sensitive to atmospheric conditions that a slight change in air movement, such as the flapping of a wing, can alter the course of the world's weather.

Spotting bad weather
Dark, cool patches can appear on the Sun's surface for about a week. These sunspots throw out debris that sometimes reaches Earth. The spots are most numerous every 11 years, and extreme weather on Earth seems to coincide with this cycle.

Global warming
Many gases and smoke particles from modern industry hang in the air. This can impact the weather. Carbon dioxide from fossil fuels is contributing to an increase in the world's temperature. This "global warming" could upset weather balances, bringing more storms and rising sea levels.

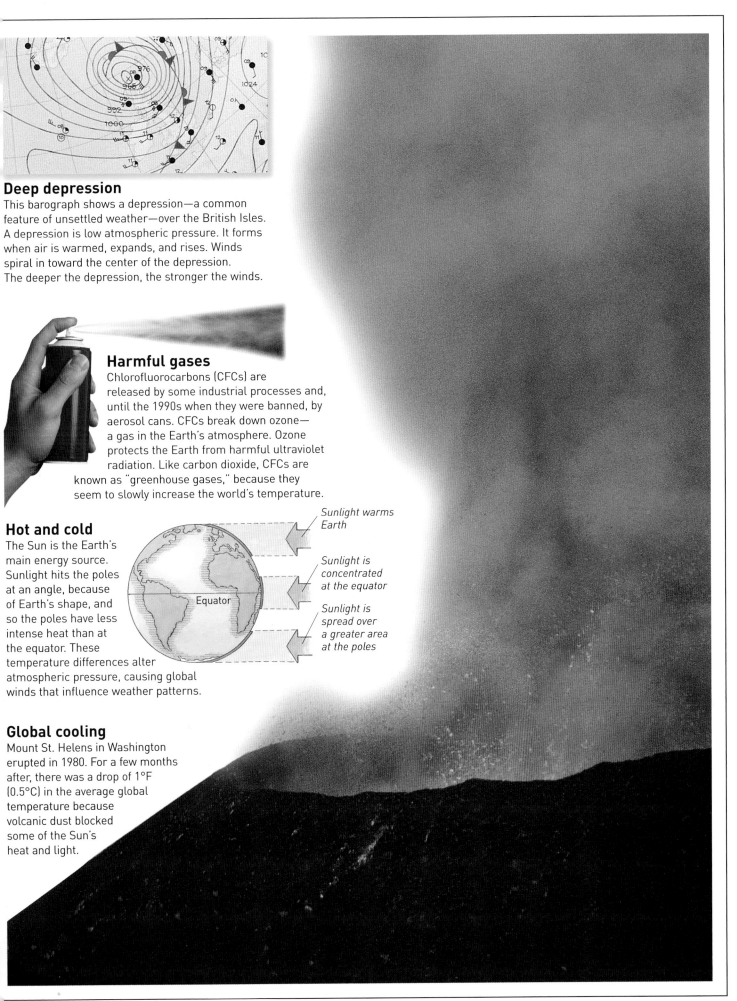

Deep depression

This barograph shows a depression—a common feature of unsettled weather—over the British Isles. A depression is low atmospheric pressure. It forms when air is warmed, expands, and rises. Winds spiral in toward the center of the depression. The deeper the depression, the stronger the winds.

Harmful gases

Chlorofluorocarbons (CFCs) are released by some industrial processes and, until the 1990s when they were banned, by aerosol cans. CFCs break down ozone—a gas in the Earth's atmosphere. Ozone protects the Earth from harmful ultraviolet radiation. Like carbon dioxide, CFCs are known as "greenhouse gases," because they seem to slowly increase the world's temperature.

Hot and cold

The Sun is the Earth's main energy source. Sunlight hits the poles at an angle, because of Earth's shape, and so the poles have less intense heat than at the equator. These temperature differences alter atmospheric pressure, causing global winds that influence weather patterns.

Equator

Sunlight warms Earth

Sunlight is concentrated at the equator

Sunlight is spread over a greater area at the poles

Global cooling

Mount St. Helens in Washington erupted in 1980. For a few months after, there was a drop of 1°F (0.5°C) in the average global temperature because volcanic dust blocked some of the Sun's heat and light.

Severe winds

Strong winds can wreak havoc. Their force depends on their speed. The fastest winds at ground level are in hurricanes and tornadoes; higher in the atmosphere are even faster winds—jet streams—that help to distribute the Sun's heat around the world. Global winds are caused by the Sun heating parts of the Earth differently, while local winds are caused by regional changes in temperature and pressure.

All at sea
In 1805, British naval commander Francis Beaufort devised a system for estimating wind speeds at sea. The Beaufort Scale assigns names and numbers to 12 different strengths of wind. It is still used today.

Standing tall
This model shows the 2,755-ft (840-m) tall Millennium Tower proposed for Tokyo, Japan. An important feature for a skyscraper is wind resistance. This tower is encircled by a steel frame to strengthen it and protect it from winds.

Architectural model of Millennium Tower, Tokyo

Head faces in the direction from which the wind is blowing

Weather vane
Weather vanes are perhaps the oldest meteorological instruments. This rooster's tail swings around as the wind changes direction and points the head toward the wind. A reading is taken of the direction from which the wind blows.

Flying in the wind
In March 1999, balloonists Bertrand Piccard and Brian Jones became the first to fly a hot-air balloon nonstop around the world. Their balloon, *Breitling Orbiter 3*, was sometimes assisted by jet-stream winds, blowing up to 185 mph (300 kph).

Windswept
Wind and sand erosion have carved these sandstone rocks. If severe winds blow across the rocks, sweeping up sand, dense and dangerous sandstorms can occur.

Wind vane to show direction

Cups spin around—their speed depends on wind strength

Rotors turn wind vane into the wind

Average wind speed is recorded as the cylinder rotates

A man struggles on Chicago's Wabash Avenue Bridge in fierce winds

Wind recorder
This anemometer records wind speed and direction over a period of time. To understand how the wind works, forecasters need to take as many measurements as possible.

Weathered sandstone, Colorado Plateau, Utah

The windy city
Chicago is on Lake Michigan, where inland and lake air mix. The atmospheric pressure of these air masses is different, and so winds batter Chicago as they collide.

Swing bridge
Strong gusts caused the Tacoma Narrows Bridge in Washington to swing in 1940. Eventually, the bridge collapsed. Since the winds were not hurricane strength, the bridge's design was blamed.

Thunderous storms

Huge amounts of energy are released in the rain, winds, thunder, and lightning that accompany thunderstorms. The most energetic storms create hail or tornadoes. The source of energy is the Sun, which causes water to evaporate; the resulting warm, moist air rises and cools, creating a cumulonimbus cloud. The rising current of air (an updraft) may travel more than 60 mph (100 kph). When rain or hail falls, a downdraft of cooler air causes gusty winds.

Letting go
Tornadoes, lightning, and waterspouts often occur during severe storms as thunderclouds quickly release energy.

View from the air
This photograph, taken from a spacecraft orbiting Earth, shows how a system of storms can develop when cold, dry air undercuts warm, moist air, lifting it to form pockets of rising air. These pockets show up as thunderheads.

Water carrier
A thunderhead is a towering cumulonimbus cloud. It may reach a height of 7.5 miles (12 km), while its base may loom just 3,300 ft (1,000 m) above ground. It usually contains about 11,000 tons (10,000 metric tons) of water.

Falls of thunder

Thunder as a demon

Drumstick to beat out the sound of thunder

Thunder

In Japan's Shinto religion, many forces of nature are worshiped as gods, known as *kami*. This *kami* of thunder is shown as a strong man beating his drum.

Japanese thunder god

○ Ice particles
● Snowflakes
● Water drops

Hot, moist air rises

Heavy rain and hail

Cloud runs out of energy

Life of a storm

A thunderstorm develops when an updraft (red arrows) of warm, moist air forms a cloud as the moisture evaporates from the air. Water vapor releases heat as it condenses. This heat warms the air more and causes it to rise higher. The storm subsides when the air cools, and the downdraft (green arrows) disperses the cloud.

Summer storms

Thunderstorms often occur after a hot day, when air warmed by the ground rises quickly into cooling air. Dense thunderclouds absorb almost all the light that falls on them. This is why they appear black.

Cloud stops rising and spreads as it hits a cold, dry layer of atmospheric air

Supercell

Most thunderstorms begin as cells (pockets) of rising air. A "supercell" is a very large, energetic cell in which air rises more quickly, carrying huge amounts of water into the cloud. Supercells create tornadoes and waterspouts.

Supercell storm cloud in Texas

Strong updrafts carry wisps of cloud into the atmosphere

Ice crystals and water

Air is drawn in at the cloud's base

17

Twisting tornadoes

Tornadoes have many names, including whirlwinds and twisters. These high-speed spiraling winds leave a trail of destruction and are a bit of a mystery. They seem to develop at the base of thunderclouds, as warm, moist air rises and passes through colder air. This draws winds that are already circulating in the storm into a high-speed whirl. The pressure at a tornado's center is lower than it is at the edges, creating a funnel that sucks up everything in its path.

A tornado funnel appears at the base of a thundercloud

1 Wall of cloud
These photographs show how a tornado develops. Its funnel descends from a thundercloud above. A column of cloud then forms as moisture as the air condenses in the low pressure inside the tornado.

Swirling black thundercloud indicates the start of a tornado

Funnel changes color as it picks up debris

2 Dusty debris
This tornado is passing over dusty farmland. The base of the tornado is therefore obscured by dust picked up by the rising air and swirling winds.

Liquid funnel
When a tornado passes over water, the updraft at its center sucks up water, forming a waterspout. A waterspout's wind speeds are much less than an ordinary tornado's because of the weight of the water it carries.

Funnel narrows as the tornado's energy diminishes

3 Losing power
Energy from the tornado's winds throws debris into the air. As the tornado loses energy, it slows down. The funnel will then shrink back into the thundercloud from which it was born.

Animal rain
When a tornado passes over water, small animals may be lifted into the air, only to rain down once the tornado loses its energy.

Spin cycle
The writhing funnel of rapidly spinning air descends to the ground from the base of a supercell. At a tornado's heart, a low-pressure vortex acts like a huge vacuum cleaner, sucking up air and anything on the ground.

Kicking up dust
Dust devils are common in desert regions. Although less energetic and less destructive than tornadoes, they are created in the same way. The circling winds typically reach speeds of about 25 mph (40 kph).

Tornado force

The swirling winds of a tornado are among the most destructive forces in nature, with speeds of up to 300 mph (500 kph). A violent tornado will destroy everything in its path. Most of the world's destructive tornadoes occur during summer in the American Midwest, where cold air from Canada in the north sits atop warm, moist air from the Gulf of Mexico to the south. This region is often called Tornado Alley. Predicting where and when tornadoes will occur is extremely difficult.

Towering

The destructive vortex (spinning center) of a tornado is usually about 1 mile (2 km) wide. Dust or objects at ground level are lifted high into the air and flung sideways, or kept in the air and deposited when the tornado winds down. Tornadoes typically travel at 35 mph (55 kph).

Venetian blind twisted by a tornado

Tornado funnel descends from a thundercloud

Blind panic

Much of a tornado's destruction is caused by the sudden drop in pressure that it brings. This window exploded outward when a tornado went by because air pressure inside the room was higher than outside it.

Door sucked out of a window by the tornado's force

Tornado Alley

This map shows the area in the US known as Tornado Alley, which includes parts of Kansas, Oklahoma, and Missouri. The region experiences several hundred tornadoes a year; tornadoes claim about 100 lives each year in the US.

CANADA

UNITED STATES

Kansas · · Missouri
· Oklahoma

MEXICO

Areas most at risk from tornadoes

Blown away

In March 1994, a torndado ripped the roof off this church in Piedmont, Virginia, surprising the congregation during a service.

In a twist

Tornado winds traveling at more than 250 mph (400 kph) picked up this truck and hurled it down again, leaving behind a mess of twisted steel and showing the incredible power of a tornado.

Dust and debris are swept up as the tornado moves along

Twisting column of cloud

Swirling vortex

A tornado rips apart a house

Chasing storms

In the US, when a "tornado watch" warning is issued, storm chasers pursue tornadoes to learn more about them.

Circles of mystery

For centuries, unexplained circles of flattened crops have appeared in fields across the world. Some people believe that tornadoes are responsible, but this is unlikely, since tornadoes do not hover over one spot for long enough.

Strange tales

A chicken in Alabama is reported to have survived tornado winds of about 125 mph (200 kph), which stripped it of its tail feathers.

Measuring tornadoes

Meteorologists use an anemometer to measure wind speeds accurately, but getting one inside a tornado is dangerous, and, because tornadoes move, it is difficult to get accurate readings. Previously, meteorologists categorized tornadoes based on estimated wind speed and damage caused. Today, though, the Doppler weather radar accurately measures wind speeds inside a tornado.

Path of a tornado
Most tornadoes travel at 20–50 mph (30–80 kph). This image shows the path of devastation left by a tornado in Oklahoma in 1999.

Doppler on wheels
Doppler radar, mounted on a truck to get close to the tornado, measures wind speed in a tornado without equipment breaking or anyone getting hurt. Microwaves directed at the tornado's edge bounce off water droplets carried by the wind. Computers in the truck then determine the speed at which the droplets are moving.

Radar dish sends out and receives microwaves

DOW3
DOPPLER ON WHEELS

etsuya (Ted) Fujita (1920–1998)

1971, this severe weather expert designed the Fujita (F)
cale, which categorizes tornadoes based on the damage
ey cause. Today, most countries use the Enhanced Fujita
F) Scale. Meteorologists in Britain use the TORRO (T) Scale.

Portable TOTO

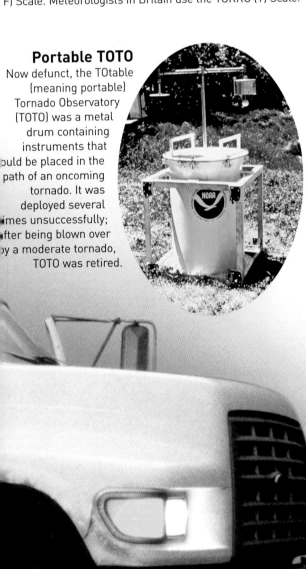

Now defunct, the TOtable
(meaning portable)
Tornado Observatory
(TOTO) was a metal
drum containing
instruments that
ould be placed in the
path of an oncoming
tornado. It was
deployed several
imes unsuccessfully;
fter being blown over
y a moderate tornado,
TOTO was retired.

Enhanced Fujita Scale

Meteorologists in the US and Canada began using the Enhanced
Fujita (EF) Scale, which runs from EF0 to EF5, in 2007. Several other
countries also use it. It gives more accurate wind speed estimates.

EF0: Minor Damage

The 65–85 mph
(105–137 kph)
winds can uproot
shallow-rooted
trees and damage
chimneys.

EF1: Moderate Damage

Winds of
86–110 mph
(138–177 kph)
overturn mobile
homes and damage
roofs and windows.

EF2: Considerable Damage

The 111–135 mph
(178–217 kph)
winds can tear off
roofs, uproot large
trees, and lift cars
off the ground.

EF3: Severe Damage

Intense 136–165 mph
(218–266 kph) winds
damage well
constructed
buildings, and can
overturn trains.

EF4: Devastating Damage

Wind speeds
of 166–200 mph
(267–322 kph) can
ruin houses and lift
cars, blowing them
long distances.

EF5: Incredible Damage

Wind speeds of
more than 200 mph
(322 kph) are very
rare but are able to
detach houses from
their foundations.

Lightning strikes

Nearly 2,000 thunderstorms occur at any one time across the Earth. Their most impressive feature is lightning, caused by an electric charge that builds up inside a thundercloud. Air inside the cloud rises at speeds of up to 60 mph (100 kph) and carries tiny ice crystals to the top of the cloud. These rub against hail pellets as they rise. The ice crystals become positively charged; the hail becomes negatively charged. A lightning bolt is a huge spark that neutralizes the electric charges.

Stormy god
Before scientists explained weather patterns, many cultures believed weather to be controlled by gods. The Norse god Thor was believed to make thunderbolts with his hammer.

Fossilized lightning bolt

Sand sculpture
This fossil is sand that has melted and then solidified in the path of a typical 54,000°F (30,000°C) bolt of lightning. The resulting mineral is fulgurite.

Bright spark
During a storm in 1752, American politician and scientist Benjamin Franklin flew a kite with metal items on its string. Sparks from the items showed electricity had passed along the wet string.

Personal safety
The Franklin wire was invented by Benjamin Franklin in 1753. The metallic wire, hung from a hat or umbrella, dragged on the ground to divert lightning from the wearer.

Lightning rods
Tall buildings, such as the Eiffel Tower in Paris, France, are regularly hit by lightning. Metal rods (called lightning rods) attached to the buildings conduct the electricity to the ground.

Lightning rods were all the rage in Paris, 1778

This tree has been torn apart by lightning

Quick as a flash

Lightning, such as the successive flashes of this storm, begins as a "leader stroke" at the base of a thundercloud and forms a path of charged atoms. Electric charges race along this path, producing a bright glow and making the air heat up rapidly and expand. This creates a shock wave—a loud thunderclap.

Cloud illuminated from within by a lightning bolt

Lightning force

The power of lightning can demolish a building or kill a person or animal. Trees are vulnerable to lightning strikes because the moist layer below the bark acts as a conductor.

Sky lights

Most lightning bolts occur within a cloud. A powerful electric current passes between the positively charged top of the cloud and its negatively charged base.

Hailstorms

Balls of ice called hailstones are produced inside a thundercloud. The strong air currents force lumps of ice up and down the cloud. With each upward movement the hailstones collect another layer of ice, until they are too big to be lifted again by the up-currents. The stronger the up-current, the heavier a hailstone can become. Heavy hailstones can be life-threatening, but any hailstorm can cause damage. One of the worst storms was in Munich, Germany, in July 1984, with financial losses around $1 billion.

Combating hail in cotton fields in the Fergana Valley, Russia

Cloud bursting
To save their crops from hail damage, the Russians fire chemical substances into thunderclouds, making potential hail fall as harmless rain. This has saved vast prairies of grain that would have otherwise been flattened by hail within minutes.

Heavy storm
Hailstones are usually about the size of a pea. They bounce when they hit a hard surface and tend to settle on the ground. But hailstones vary in size, and storms in severity. In the US alone, a hailstorm can cause property damage of more than $500 million and crop damage of $300 million.

Corn crop destroyed by a severe hailstorm

Hail Alley
A belt of land in the US spanning from Texas to Montana is known as "Hail Alley" and regularly experiences severe hailstorms. Little has been done, however, to explore methods of crop protection.

Vehicles pelted by hail during a storm in Texas in May 1977

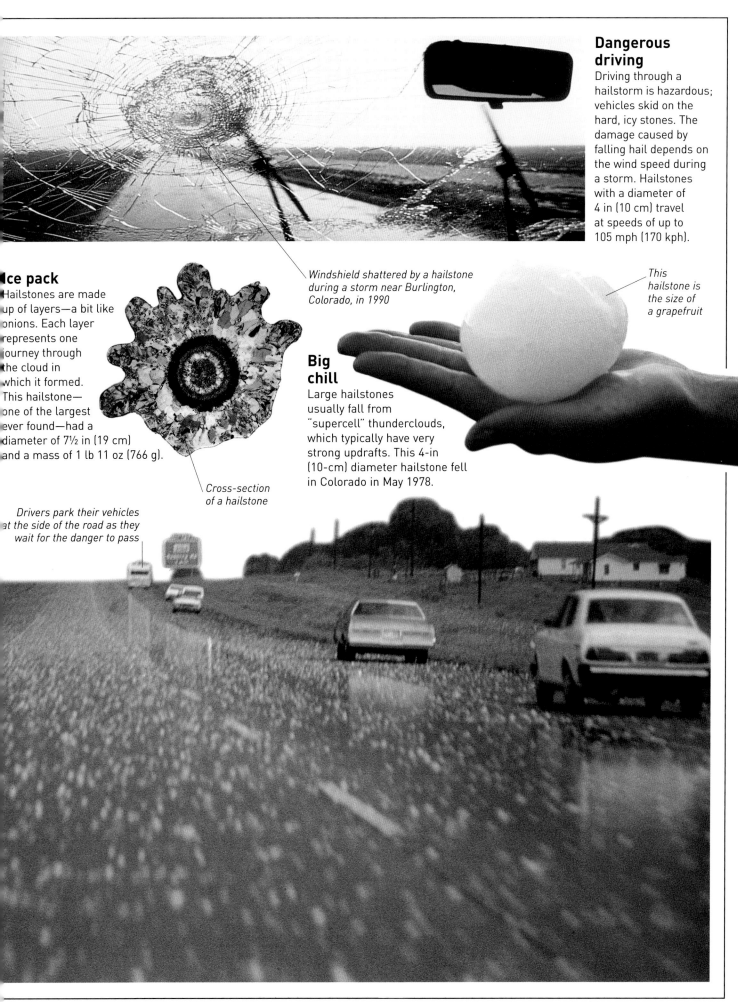

Dangerous driving

Driving through a hailstorm is hazardous; vehicles skid on the hard, icy stones. The damage caused by falling hail depends on the wind speed during a storm. Hailstones with a diameter of 4 in (10 cm) travel at speeds of up to 105 mph (170 kph).

Windshield shattered by a hailstone during a storm near Burlington, Colorado, in 1990

This hailstone is the size of a grapefruit

Ice pack

Hailstones are made up of layers—a bit like onions. Each layer represents one journey through the cloud in which it formed. This hailstone— one of the largest ever found—had a diameter of 7½ in (19 cm) and a mass of 1 lb 11 oz (766 g).

Cross-section of a hailstone

Big chill

Large hailstones usually fall from "supercell" thunderclouds, which typically have very strong updrafts. This 4-in (10-cm) diameter hailstone fell in Colorado in May 1978.

Drivers park their vehicles at the side of the road as they wait for the danger to pass

Hurricane alert

Hurricanes, or tropical cyclones, are known as cyclones in the Indian Ocean and typhoons in the Pacific. They are huge, rotating storms with winds of up to 215 mph (350 kph), heavy rain, and stormy seas. In the warm seas of the tropics (near the equator), a hurricane begins as heated air expands and rises, creating an area of low pressure. Surrounding air moves toward the low pressure and spins due to Earth's rotation.

Warning
The destruction from a hurricane can be reduced if a warning is given. These flags are a hurricane alert.

19th-century aneroid barometer

Many buildings were wrecked when a hurricane hit Albany, Georgia, in 1940

Gale force
The destructive force of a hurricane comes largely from its strong winds. As more and more air is drawn in toward the center of the storm, the spiraling winds' speed increases.

Under pressure
The atmospheric pressure, measured by a barometer, is very low in a hurricane. Changes in pressure can help predict approaching storms.

Wheeled warning
In a Bangladeshi village, where few people have radios or televisions, this man is using a megaphone to warn of a hurricane

Water, water...
Under the low-pressure air at the center of a storm, the sea level bulges to as much as 3 ft (1 m) higher than normal. This "storm surge" adds to the flooding along coastlines, which causes most of the deaths from hurricanes.

A community in Bangladesh waits for a hurricane threat to pass

Stilts raise this specially built cyclone shelter above the ground

Safety on stilts
Floods are common during a hurricane, caused by heavy rains and high ocean waves. This shelter is raised so flood waters can pass beneath it without endangering lives.

Spinning cyclones

Hurricanes are tropical cyclones. A cyclone is an area of low-pressure air with winds that spiral inward—clockwise in the southern hemisphere, counterclockwise in the northern. They move west from their origin near the equator, but can curve east as they cross the tropics.

Northern hemisphere

Equator

NEW GUINEA

AUSTRALIA

Southern hemisphere

View from above

Hurricanes form where the seawater is above 80°F (27°C). A low pressure forms. Once winds reach 39 mph (62 kph), it is a tropical storm. When they reach 74 mph (118 kph), it is a hurricane and picks up 2.2 billion tons (2 billion metric tons) of water, as vapor, from the ocean each day. This vapor condenses to form clouds. The eye, or center, of a hurricane is very calm, while all around it are thick clouds and high-speed winds.

The eye of a storm can be up to 30 miles (50 km) wide

Satellite view of Hurricane Emilia (1994)

Devastation

Some regions are more prone to hurricanes than others. Areas outside the tropics—more than 1,500 miles (2,500 km) from the equator—are much less at risk than tropical regions because the seas are cooler, providing less energy to fuel hurricanes. Hurricanes bring huge waves, known as storm surges, which cause the biggest loss of lives. But it is the strong winds that cause the greatest destruction.

The hurricane of 1900 demolished this school in Galveston, but the desks stayed screwed to the floor.

American tragedy
One of the deadliest hurricanes in the US struck the coastal city of Galveston, Texas, in September 1900. More than 12,000 people died, 2,600 homes were destroyed, and about 10,000 people were left homeless.

Hurricane David's powerful winds lifted this plane and deposited it on top of a hangar.

Hanging around
The Dominican Republic was struck by dangerous and destructive Hurricane David in August 1979. The storm reached speeds of 172 mph (277 kph) and lasted two weeks, bombarding the coastline with huge waves; 1,300 people lost their lives.

In the bunker
Flood waters produced by Hurricane Hugo in 1989 swept this boat from the harbor to a nearby golf course. Hugo hit the Virgin Islands before moving over warm water, where it gained energy, and then struck South Carolina.

A low, flat, and well secured roof helped this house to survive almost entirely intact

Reduced to rubble
In April 1991, Cyclone 2B hit Bangladesh; 150-mph (240-kph) winds reduced homes to rubble, and a 20-ft (6-m) tidal wave claimed more than 140,000 lives.

Wave power
Due to low atmospheric pressure at a hurricane's heart, there is a swell of water up to 10 ft (3 m) high. If it moves close to land, the swell becomes a huge wave, flooding vast areas, such as when Hurricane Floyd struck the US in 1999.

Without warning
In late December 1974, Cyclone Tracy formed 300 miles (500 km) northeast of the Australian coast. The local Tropical Cyclone Warning Center thought the hurricane would miss land, but early on Christmas Day, it turned and hit Darwin. About 90 percent of the buildings were destroyed, leaving half of its 40,000 people homeless; more than 20,000 people were airlifted out.

I will survive
In August 1992, Hurricane Andrew devastated the Bahamas, and Louisiana and Florida in the US. It caused 52 deaths and about $22 billion worth of damage. The lucky resident of this house in Florida, however, was proud to have survived the fierce storms.

Rainbands

Clockwise outflow

Eye of the storm

Spirals counter-clockwise

Hurricane formation

Hurricanes develop above warm ocean waters. Moist, rising air causes an area of very low pressure. Surrounding air spirals inward and forms curved clouds called rainbands. Air from the eye (center) flows out above the storm.

Hurricane strikes

It usually takes several days for storms over tropical oceans to develop into hurricanes. By studying how hurricanes develop, meteorologists can better predict which storm will become a hurricane, where it is likely to go, and how powerful it might be, helping emergency services to prepare better, and giving people more time to evacuate

Center of the storm is a low-pressure area

1 Hurricane trigger

These satellite images show Hurricane Katrina's development in 2005. The storm began forming on August 23 in warm waters over the Bahamas. A center of low pressure began drawing in air.

Rainbands form as air swirls in toward the center

2 A swirling mass

The storm absorbed more energy from the warm water in the Gulf of Mexico and formed huge spiral rainbands. On August 25, it moved northwest and passed over Florida and back into the Gulf.

Hurricane's eye is calm

3 Mature stage

By August 29, the storm had a well-defined eye. It hit land again in Louisiana, where flooding and high winds caused damage worth billions of dollars.

Gusty wind
This picture shows the conditions beneath a hurricane's spiraling clouds. The high winds are caused by huge difference in atmospheric pressure. As the air spirals inward, it speeds up

Trees bend over in the strong wind

Dish reflector

Hurricane reader

Mounted on aircraft that fly over storm clouds, the High-Altitude Imaging Wind and Rain Airborne Profiler (HIWRAP) uses radar to measure wind speeds around hurricanes, which helps scientists understand and make more accurate predictions about these storms.

Two "transceivers" transmit and receive radar beams

Floodwaters in New Orleans

Hurricane Katrina was the costliest and one of the five most deadly hurricanes in US history. Almost 2,000 people died, and damage costs were at least $81 billion. The worst-hit area was New Orleans, where the storm surge—a bulge of seawater— poured over the levees (flood barriers).

Hurricane Wilma, 2005, near Cancun, Mexico

Driving is extremely hazardous in hurricane conditions

Fog and smog

When air is full of moisture and the temperature drops, fog may occur. Fog is cloud at ground level, made up of tiny water droplets. Fog is translucent, like tracing paper, since it scatters light. Thick fog reduces visibility, and accidents on the roads, at sea, or in the air are common. Foghorns or radar locate ships and planes; traffic signals and lighthouses can guide them to safety. When fog combines with smoke, thick and dangerous smog may form.

Pea-soupers
Until the 1960s Clean Air Act forced the use of "smokeless fuel," people in London, England, suffered dangerously bad smog that led to breathing problems. Nicknamed "pea-soupers," the smog was caused by burning coal

Takeoff
During World War II, kerosene was burned to provide heat to clear fog from airport runways. The heat turned water droplets in fog into invisible vapor. It worked, but was expensive and dangerous.

Airport staff member ignites fog burners

Water catchers
For residents of Chungungo village, a dry part of Chile, frequent fog is a blessing. These long, plastic fences outside the village catch water from fog that blows in from the sea, providing much of the village's water supply.

Sulfurous smog hangs over Christchurch, New Zealand

Cleaning up the air
Sulfurous smog hangs in the air above many cities. It is produced when smoke combines with fog, and is a danger to health and traffic. Today, sulfurous smogs are less common due to cleaner fuels, but equally deadly is "photochemical smog" caused by sunlight combining with air pollutants.

Gas container

Loud noise travels through this horn

Sounding the alarm

Thick sea-fog hides boats from each other. Gas released from this foghorn makes a loud noise that can be heard clearly through the fog to help prevent collisions. Large ships have huge, deafening foghorns that can be heard over many miles.

Lighting the way

Before the invention of radar, sailors had no way of seeing in thick sea-fogs. Lighthouses warned sailors of the dangers ahead, guiding ships away from rocks or shallow water by flashing a powerful beam of light during fogs and at night.

Golden Gate Bridge in San Francisco is hidden beneath a blanket of fog

Fog City

San Francisco is known as "Fog City" because of its summer fog that occurs when warm, moist air meets the cool water that travels into San Francisco Bay from down the coast.

High seas

Strong winds constantly disturb the surface of the oceans, producing waves that break on coastlines. During severe storms and hurricanes, seawater can cause flooding along the coast and ships to sink. Scientists fear that global warming may cause more of the the ice caps to melt, resulting in a rise in sea levels, increasing flood risks, and coastal erosion in many places.

In deep water
High seas have dangerous waves that can sink ships. Rescue helicopters help survivors, hovering above the sea while a rescuer is lowered on a winch to lift survivors from the water.

A rescuer is lowered to the sea by a search-and-rescue helicopter

Collapsed coastal road caused by wave erosion

Tearing along
Crashing waves wreak havoc on coastlines, dissolving rock and breaking off parts of cliffs. The stormier and higher the sea, the greater the erosion. If sea levels rise, so will erosion and flood risks.

Holding back
The Thames River Barrier aims to protect London, England, from flooding until at least 2050. Ten huge gates can be raised when sea levels surge, preventing water from traveling up the river.

Tsunami
Often mistakenly called tidal waves, tsunamis are triggered by earthquakes beneath the seabed and can devastate areas, such as here on Okushiri Island, Japan.

Stormy sea
Hurricane Hugo hit the West Indies and southeastern US in 1989 with a surge 6 ft (2 m) high. This rose to 18 ft (6 m) in some places, where the water was funneled up along valleys.

Wall of water

Wind blows across the ocean surface, making the water swing up and down, back and forth, forming waves. When waves approach the shore, where the sea is shallower, they move more slowly, and their crests get taller and closer together. Eventually, the waves topple over, forming breakers.

This huge, plunging wave is on the verge of breaking

Snowstorms

Extremely cold conditions can endanger lives. When the temperature falls below freezing—32°F (0°C)—snow settles on the ground. Sometimes, wind blows the snow into piles, called snowdrifts. Snow and strong winds cause blizzards, which reduce visibility. Snowflakes are clumps of ice crystals made inside a cloud when water vapor freezes around specks of mineral dust. Ice storms occur when water in the air freezes to form icy fog at ground level.

Piled high
Snow has piled up against the side of this house in Derbyshire, England. Snowdrifts such as this form when snow carried by the wind is stopped in its tracks by an obstacle.

Whiteout
Blizzards have forced these drivers to stop their cars. If they remain in their vehicles, they can be found more easily, but they risk freezing. One person froze to death during this snowstorm near Caen, France.

Ice crystal from a snowflake

What is snow?
The ice crystals that make up snowflakes are tiny, but their beautiful symmetrical shapes can be viewed through a microscope. Their growth depends on temperature, humidity, and air currents in a cloud. These conditions are never identical, and so no two snowflakes are the same.

Clearing the way
Snowplows keep major roads clear of heavy snow, and cars use tire chains for better grip. A sudden snowfall can cause chaos; tires easily lose their grip and accidents are common.

Blade of a snowplow clearing a road in France

RENAULT

Frozen drips

Icicles form as water drips from ridges, such as rooftops or tree branches. A small amount of each drip freezes while the rest drips off. Gradually, drip by drip, an icicle builds up.

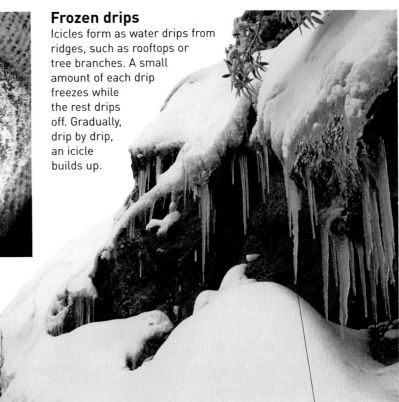

Wind chill

This man's face-warmer froze as he shoveled snow in Milwaukee, Wisconsin. During this severe winter storm in December 1995, the temperature was -31°F (-35°C), but the "wind chill" made it feel like -94°F (-70°C). Wind chill occurs on a windy day, when heat passes from your warm body to cold air more quickly than on a calm day, making it feel colder than it really is.

Icicles hang from a cliff during an ice storm in Arizona

Staying indoors

Extremely cold weather can force people to stay indoors for safety and warmth. Vehicles may become frozen, such as this car in northeastern Canada, when the temperature dropped to -20°F (-29°C). During this storm, trees fell down under the weight of ice, and thousands of cattle froze to death.

Watching for signs

Most mountain resorts warn of avalanche danger. By examining the snow, experts can tell when an area is at risk, but not where and when an avalanche will strike.

This crack marks the start of a slab avalanche

Avalanche

One of the most dangerous things in mountainous areas is an avalanche, when huge amounts of snow slide down a mountain, burying buildings and the people in them. The Swiss Alps is one of the areas most at risk, with about 10,000 avalanches every year. Avalanches occur after snow builds up on mountain slopes in layers— a new layer laid during each snowfall. When the layers are unstable, an avalanche can be triggered by strong winds, vibrations, or temperature changes. Anyone caught under this cold, heavy blanket needs immediate rescue.

Under cover

In areas where avalanches are common, protective sheds are often built over major roads. The sheds allow avalanches to pass over the road, keeping the road clear.

Breaking away

Most avalanches occur when melted snow breaks away as a large slab. As it begins to move, cracks (fissures) show in the snow, usually on bulging slopes and snow that's overhanging clifftops.

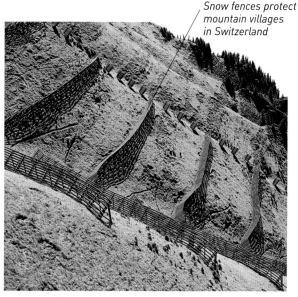

Snow fences protect mountain villages in Switzerland

Bang, bang

When a mass of snow is ready, an avalanche can be set off by the slightest vibration. In places threatened by serious avalanches, explosives are used to set them off deliberately before too much snow builds up

An avalanche forecaster checks the stability of snow layers

Snow stoppers

Sturdy trees on a mountainside can absorb some of the energy of sliding snow. Artificial barriers made of wood, concrete, or metal can provide similar protection.

Look closely

Avalanche forecasters build snow pits to examine snow layers. An avalanche is more likely if a layer contains air or is made up of graupel (ice pellets). These pellets can roll over each other, allowing slabs of snow above to break away.

Snowy river

Airborne powder avalanches, such as this one, occur soon after a fresh snowfall. They flow like water, throwing up vast splashes on the valley floor. The high-speed mass of snow smothers everything in its path and compresses the air in front of it, creating loud tremors.

A rescue dog searches for survivors in the Swiss Alps

Sniff search

Specially trained dogs help to locate people trapped under heavy snow after avalanches. With their highly developed sense of smell, dogs are more efficient than any electronic sensor, although off-trail skiers do carry personal radio beacons.

Floods and landslides

Flooding causes more than a third of all deaths from natural disasters. A flash flood occurs when rain is heavy and rivers break their banks, or sewers quickly become overwhelmed. In the Indian subcontinent, seasonal winds called monsoons bring torrential rain and floods every summer. When torrential rain combines with high tides and strong winds, coastal areas are particularly at risk. When large volumes of rainwater mix with soil, the muddy mixture can slip down a hill—a landslide.

Noah's Ark
According to the Bible, God was unhappy with how humans were living, and so decided to kill most of the human race with a 40-day flood. God chose Noah and his family to survive. He told him to build an ark and take a male and female of each species.

Damage caused by the Johnstown flash flood

Dam buster
After heavy rain on May 31, 1889, a dam near Johnstown, Pennsylvania, collapsed. The north of the city was swept away by thousands of tons of water, and 2,209 people died.

Rice
Monsoon rains on the island of Java, Indonesia, are vital for rice crops. But sometimes heavy rains bring floods that endanger lives and precious crops.

A farmer in Java tries to save a rice crop from the floods

Breaking the bank
During monsoon season, the Ganges River in south Asia often bursts its banks. The floods of July and August 1998 were the worst in 20 years, submerging up to two-thirds of Bangladesh. About 1,500 people died, mostly from snakebites or waterborne diseases.

Muddy river
In May 1998, after two days of torrential rain in Quindici, Italy, local rivers burst their banks. Muddy water flooded the town, leaving 3,000 homeless and killing about 50 people—many of them buried under a thick layer of mud.

Landslide debris on a 100-ft- (30-m) high clay slope

Watery intruder
Storm waters broke into this seaside home in Florida during Hurricane Andrew in 1991. Fierce winds and a surge of high water are caused by the low atmospheric pressure of the hurricane's center.

Moving mud
When water and mud mix on a hillside, gravity pulls the mud and anything else in its path downward. This hotel in Scarborough, England, slipped downhill during a landslide in June 1993.

Home upturned by a powerful storm surge

Storm on the waterfront
These residents of the Florida Keys sought refuge as Hurricane George, which had already devastated some Carribean islands, hit the coastline in 1998. They battled against 90-mph (140-kph) winds and a surge of water from the Atlantic.

Heat waves

A heat wave is a spell of unusually warm and humid weather. People can suffer from heatstroke—dizziness and confusion, nausea, and faster than normal heartbeats—which, in extreme cases, can kill. Sweating helps cool the body, but sweat evaporates more slowly in humid air. Despite the humidity, the land can be very dry, so wildfires are a danger.

Climate change

Average temperatures are rising. In this 2008 map, orange and red show where temperatures were higher than average; areas cooler than average are blue. As temperatures rise, heat waves are becoming more common

Urban heat islands

Temperatures in cities are usually a degree or two higher (shown in this map as yellow and white) than less built-up areas, because concrete absorbs more heat than vegetation. As a result, people in cities are at highest risk of health issues during heat waves

Sun shade

During a heat wave, intense sunlight heats the body, increasing the risk of heatstroke and causing painful sunburn on the skin, which has similar symptoms to heatstroke. These people are using an umbrella for shade during a heat wave in Shanghai, China, in 2013.

Wildfires

In June 2012, the northwestern US experienced one of its worst recorded heat waves. Record temperatures and very low rainfall created conditions for wildfires, like this one in the heavily forested state of Montana.

Europe 2003

People enjoyed the sunshine during the 2003 European heat wave. It was not all fun, though: experts estimated that the heat wave caused around 70,000 deaths, and the accompanying drought brought crop failures.

Moscow 2010

In the summer of 2010, much of eastern Europe experienced record high temperatures. Wildfires raged for weeks in the countryside around Moscow, Russia. Smoke filled the city's air, causing smog—many inhabitants wore face masks, but the death rate in the city was twice the norm for the month.

Search for food

Heat waves can cause hardship for wildlife, as wildfires destroy their habitats and food sources. This deer is searching for food in a national park near Athens, Greece, after a heat wave in the summer of 2007.

A forest fire burning the side of a mountain in Montana

Deadly droughts

Any region lacking in water because of lower-than-normal rainfall is in a drought. As rivers, lakes, and soil dry up, crops fail and animals starve, leading to famine among humans. Advances in medicine, transportation, and communications in the 20th century allowed aid agencies to lessen the effects of water scarcity, but droughts are still a problem in much of Africa. Droughts are sometimes caused by human activities, such as over farming.

Skin and bones
Animal carcasses are a common sight during severe droughts. This unfortunate animal dried out before it had a chance to decay.

Powerful painting
This Aboriginal bark painting from Arnhem Land (a hot, dry part of northern Australia) was used in rain-making ceremonies. The stingray symbolizes the "watery" power that summons rain.

Animals gather around a waterhole in Namibia, southern Africa

Diminishing supply
Animals in dry climates gather around scarce pools of water, called waterholes. During a drought, more water evaporates and is drunk than is supplied by rainfall, and there are fewer plants for animals to eat, too. As a result, millions of animals can die during a drought.

War and want
One of the worst droughts was in east Africa during 2011 and 2012. After two years of very low rainfall, crops and livestock were severely affected. Millions of people suffered malnutrition, and tens of thousands died.

Fighting fire
Droughts cause disastrous forest fires, fueled by the dry leaves and wood of vegetation. Most fires start naturally, but some are caused by a careless act, such as a dropped match. Some trees have fireproof bark, or bark that peels off when ignited. Other trees will not germinate until their cones are scorched.

Blowing in the wind

Deserts are in permanent drought, and so most are covered in dry sand or sandy soil. The wind can blow dry sand grains around, causing sandstorms. Sandstorms create sand dunes, which make up much of the landscape of the hottest deserts.

Black blizzards

In the 1930s, the Great Plains of the North American Midwest suffered severe drought. Grasses in the fields had been plowed so the topsoil dried to dust and blew away in clouds. Thousands left their homes, and some died of starvation or lung disease from inhaling the dust.

Thirsty leaves

In the drylands of southwest Africa, the kokerboom tree can survive several years of drought. Its leaves shrink, having lost most of their moisture.

Cracking up

Large areas of land with no vegetation quickly suffer from drought. No plants means no water store, and no protection from winds that increase evaporation from the soil. Water helps bind soil grains; dry mud cracks, becomes brittle, and produces dust.

Lake Naivasha in Kenya, Africa, dried up from a drought

Polar extremes

The North and South poles are frozen all year round because they receive little sunlight. Around the North Pole, the Arctic has no land, only thick ice. Around the South Pole, Antarctica's land is constantly covered by snow. Strong winds in Antarctica are caused when cold air flows off steep slopes, blowing snow into a blinding blizzard. Temperatures peak at -40°F (-40°C) during the long, dark polar winters. The polar regions and their cold currents are important for global weather.

An icebreaker clears a path through the St. Lawrence River, Canada

Breaking the ice
During winter, when huge amounts of sea ice form, powerful ice-breaking ships keep waterways clear, transport vital supplies, and are research station[s]

Eye protection
Goggles protect eyes from the glare of sunlight, which is reflected by the snow.

Ice station
During summer, polar research stations house nearly 4,000 people at 42 sites. Less than 1,000 people live there in winter. By studying the weather at the poles, scientists can learn more about the Earth's weather patterns.

Get a grip
Climbing boots have a themal lining and pants clip to the tops of the boots to help retain body heat in icy conditions. Crampons (spikes) on the soles provide grip.

Tough and durable plastic outer layer

Bright red color makes the jacket stand out in a blizzard

Elasticated cuffs keep out icy winds

Spikes help to grip thick, slippery ice

Bib overalls

Fly the flag
Newly fallen snow and blizzards can bury important items. Some people plant colored flags to help them find their tents and supplies.

Pyramid tent to withstand high-speed blizzard winds

Weather station
There are automatic weather stations across the polar regions. Forecasting the weather is important for the safety of those who live and work in these hostile environments.

Weather balloon for gathering data about the atmosphere

Undergarment traps a layer of air, which is warmed by the body

Weather balloon
Equipment in this weather balloon measures the temperature and concentration of gases in the Antarctic atmosphere. These measurements help scientists test theories and make more accurate forecasts.

Waterproof nylon outer layer with goose-down stuffing

Scientists in Antarctica use a drill to extract samples from the sea ice

Time freeze
Much of the ice at the poles has been frozen for millions of years. It preserves things that were around when it froze. By studying samples, scientists can discover what the climate was like many years ago.

Wrap up
In polar climates, "extreme cold weather outfits" cover the body. Outer layers include waterproof jacket and overalls, made up of several layers of different materials—the best way to reduce heat loss.

Staying alive
Multilayered gloves protect hands, which are at most risk from freezing conditions, as the body shuts off blood to them to reduce heat loss. Severe conditions can cause frostbite.

Weather watch

With enough warning that a hurricane is going to hit, many deaths can be avoided. Hurricanes can be tracked using weather satellites, but other types of extreme weather require ground-based measurements—including wind speed, temperature, and atmospheric pressure. The data are recorded using instruments around the world, on land and at sea. Forecasters use computers to analyze data and to predict how the weather will behave. The most difficult to predict are short-lived phenomena like tornadoes and long-term conditions such as drought.

Signs from space
Geostationary satellites hover in space about 22,500 miles (36,000 km) above the equator. They record atmospheric temperature and cloud patterns of a particular region on Earth.

Solar cells power the Meteosat satellite

About 400 bumpy projections help to stabilize this balloon while in flight

Propellers sustain less damage in a storm than jet engines

Extra fuel is carried in tanks mounted on the wings

Doppler-radar dome

Round radar
Sensitive radar equipment enables weather scientists to make more accurate forecasts. The US National Weather Service relies on ground-based Doppler-radar stations to measure wind speeds and rainfall, and to calculate cloud positions.

High in the sky
Balloons are essential to weather forecasting. They carry instruments into Earth's atmosphere, and transmit readings by radio. Measurements of upper atmosphere conditions are important for predicting what the weather may do next, and for discovering more about how the weather works.

Working with the weather
A modern weather forecast involves countless measurements of temperature, air pressure, and rainfall, plus complicated mathematics. No wonder computers are used—although humans are needed to interpret it all.

From far afield
This automatic weather station is in the middle of a field. It gathers measurements of wind speed and direction, temperature, humidity, and sunlight. The more data that meteorologists can collect, the better their forecasts will be.

Instrument for recording wind speed and direction

A meteorologist downloads weather data to his portable computer

Satellite view
Infrared is heat radiation. It is not visible to human eyes, but can be detected by special cameras. The warmer something is, the more infrared it produces. A satellite picture like this helps meteorologists to measure temperature across the world's surface.

A large tailplane gives greater stability at low speed

Hurricane hunter
The meteorologists and instruments aboard this Lockheed WC-130 modified military transport airplane fly into hurricanes at an altitude of 2 miles (3 km) to help with accurate hurricane forecasts.

Satellite is carried in the rocket's nose cone

There it goes
The Geostationary Operational Environmental Satellite system (GOES) is a series of satellites that monitor Earth's entire surface (except the polar regions). This latest satellite, GOES-15, was launched on a Delta IV rocket from Cape Canaveral, Florida, in 2010.

Weather buoy

Tornado pump
Weather forecasts are available across the media, from newspapers to the Internet, and gas pumps, such as this one in the US. A built-in screen shows tornado movements and announces warnings.

Sea search
Buoys carry automatic weather stations. They drift in the sea for weeks, measuring wind speed, temperature, and humidity. It is important to monitor sea conditions because they greatly influence the Earth's climate.

Disaster relief

Extreme weather phenomena, such as storms, droughts, and floods, can cause massive destruction. When this happens, people may need help to keep them alive and well, or somewhere to stay while their homes are being repaired, or even rebuilt. Food and water supplies may be affected, too. International aid agencies provide assistance, food, and medical supplies to those who suffer due to the weather.

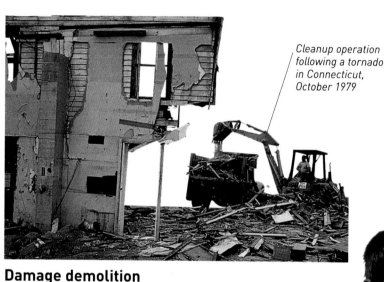

Cleanup operation following a tornado in Connecticut, October 1979

Upturned lives
A rescuer searches this upturned home following a tornado in Florida. People in the southwestern US suffer many hurricanes and tornadoes, but they can never be fully prepared. While rebuilding occurs, people are housed temporarily.

Damage demolition
This building was destroyed by a tornado. The governments of wealthy countries set aside emergency funds to pay for rebuilding work. Poorer countries often need outside aid.

Portable water
During a flood, drinking water is often cut off or in short supply. This Filipino boy is collecting fresh water from a tank.

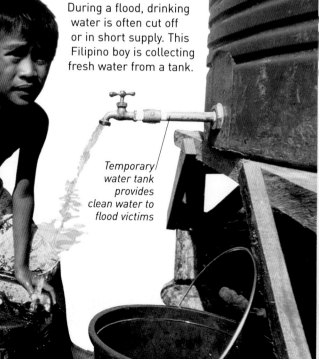

Temporary water tank provides clean water to flood victims

Mopping up
A priority in a flood is to drain excess water. Powerful pumps clear the streets; sandbags protect properties from floodwater and control the direction of the flow.

Air meals

When a natural disaster strikes a remote location, the quickest way to bring aid is to drop supplies from the air. Each of the tightly bound packages from this airplane contained flour, oil, and canned fruit. It is difficult to drop water in these packages, even though it is often what is most needed.

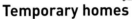

Makeshift shelters in a refugee camp in Ethiopia

Temporary homes

When drought brought famine to Ethiopia in 1989, the United Nations set up a camp in Sidamo Province, helping 45,000 people. Each family was given plastic sheeting as a temporary shelter, a sleeping mat, cooking utensils, food, and water. Refugees had to find their own cooking and building materials, putting a great strain on scarce resources.

Emergency food supplies

Disease prevention

Epidemics rapidly break out in disaster sites, and they are a common cause of death. This aid worker is spraying insecticide to kill disease-spreading mosquitoes. Insecticides that will not harm people when they filter into the water supply must be used.

All dried up

When this picture was taken, there had been no rain in the Suguta Valley, Kenya, for seven years. Famine is common during a serious drought, particularly in remote areas with few supplies. This is why food aid from charities, such as Oxfam, is important.

Nature's survivors

The world's plants and animals are well adapted to their environments. If they were not, they would soon die out, particularly in extreme climates such as deserts. Some living things are so well adapted to their surroundings that you might think they had been specially designed to live there. But living things adapt to their surroundings gradually—over many generations.

Feather coat
Snowy owls live in Arctic regions. Their soft, fluffy feathers hold lots of air, which insulates them against the cold. They even have feathers around their claws. If the weather becomes hot, snowy owls cool themselves by spreading their wings and panting.

Fat monster
The gila monster lives in Mexico and the southwestern US. In the warm, rainy season, food is plentiful, and the gila monster stores body fat, on which it can live during the cold, dry winter.

Fat stored in the tail provides energy in winter

Upside-down tree
According to myth, the strange-looking baobab tree angered the gods, who punished it by replanting it upside down. In reality, the tree has leaves for only three months a year which, along with water stored in its huge trunk, enables the tree to survive East Africa's dry season.

Drip tip of a rain-forest leaf

Useful tips
In a rain forest, about 3 ft (1 m) of rain falls each month during the rainy season. Plants depend on water to survive, but constantly wet leaves kill them. Some leaves developed "drip tips" to carry away the water.

Stemming the flow
Leaves are covered with stomata (tiny holes) that allow water to escape. As it does so, more water is drawn from the soil by the plant. Where water is scarce, plants have fewer or smaller leaves. Many cacti have no leaves at all; they are simply large stems containing water.

Some like it wet

Like all frogs, red-eyed tree frogs have moist skin. If their skin dries out, they will die, and so tree frogs thrive in the damp rain forests. They also have suckers on their feet to clamber among the branches.

Underground movers

Most amphibians need to keep their skin moist. During a drought, many stay in burrows, or a moist location like a rotting log. During a dry season, some frogs become dormant, cocooning themselves in moist mud.

Australian burrowing frog

Water hump

In the constant drought of the desert, a camel can make water from its own body fat, using a quarter of its body weight.

A camel can drink the equivalent of a bathtub full of water in just a few minutes

In a cold climate

Emperor penguins live in the harsh Antarctic all year round. Waterproof feathers and thick fat layers help them survive on land and in the icy seas. During winter, their body fat provides an essential energy source.

Overlapping, closely packed feathers keep out fierce winds

Fluffy-feathered chicks huddle for warmth

Feet are small to minimize heat loss

Climate change

A region's climate is its typical weather over 30 years. But climates can change. Ice ages—when world temperatures are very low—cause more frozen seawater, larger polar ice caps, and more land ice in the form of huge glaciers. One cause of ice ages is the varying distance between Earth and the Sun. At other times, higher than normal temperatures have wiped out civilizations. Scientists use many techniques, including examining fossils or tree rings, to "read" climate records.

Ever-changing sea

The ammonoid, or ammonite, was a shelled marine animal that once lived in warm seas. Ammonoid fossils were found in Antarctic oceans, from when Antarctica was not at the South Pole, and so not cold. Like all continents, Antarctica has drifted across Earth.

Frost fair on the Thames River in London, 181

Lost civilization

Dramatic climate change can force people out of their homes. The ancient Peublo peoples lived in these caves, in the southwest of what is now the US, until about 1280. They moved after a 23-year drought.

Mini Ice Age

Much of Europe experienced the "Little Ice Age," from 1500 to 1850. The average temperature was only a few degrees lower than normal, but rivers and seawater froze, and winters were harsh.

Thick, woolly coat provides insulation

Huge, curved ivory tusks warded off predators and probably swept aside snow when feeding

Woolly mammoth

During the last Great Ice Age, woolly mammoths lived in the icy tundra of North America, Europe, and Asia. They died out as the world's climate warmed.

Hair-covered trunk to keep out the cold

Tree circles

Trees grow thicker each year. New living wood is created in a layer beneath the bark. Each year's growth appears as a ring. The warmer the climate, the more growth and the thicker the ring. By analyzing ring width, scientists can calculate average temperatures for each year of the tree's life.

The thicker a tree ring, the warmer the climate that year

Bristlecone pines growing on the White Mountains, California

Living record

The oldest living trees are bristlecone pines, found in California and Nevada. Some are more than 4,000 years old and are a living record of the climate. Removing a thin sample allows its rings to be analyzed.

Space dust

When a huge meteorite hit Earth 50,000 years ago, millions of tons of dust were thrown into the air and stayed there for a year, reflecting much sunlight back into space. Some scientists believe this can cause reduced global temperatures.

Global warming

The world's average temperature is rising. Most climate scientists blame human activity, such as the burning of fuels. If global warming carries on at this rate, more ice at the poles will melt, causing flooding in many places next century.

A massive iceberg in Greenland dwarfs a passing fishing trawler

El Niño

Every two to 10 years, part of the Pacific Ocean becomes warmer than normal during winter, and Pacific winds change direction, blowing warm water east toward South America. This El Niño effect causes extreme weather in the tropics that can last up to four years. Outside the tropics, El Niño can cause average winter temperatures to fall and increased winter rainfall. El Niño can be predicted several months ahead, so early warnings allow farmers to alter their crops for the conditions.

Hot and cold
This map shows how El Niño affected global temperatures in 1983. The orange and red areas show warmer than normal temperatures; the blue areas, cooler than normal.

Hard times
El Niño (Spanish for "the Christ child") was so-called by Peruvian fishermen because it appears over Christmas. When El Niño winds blow warm water over the cool Peruvian seas, plankton cannot grow in the warmer water and so the fish that eat the plankton disappear. Many Peruvians depend on fishing and so suffer during El Niño.

On the rocks
Sea lions and seabirds off the western coast of South America often starve during El Niño because they feed on the fish that thrive on the cold-water plankton. When El Niño hits, the cool waters are pushed down. The fish swim deeper—out of reach.

Warm and wet
The 1998 El Niño causes floods in Kenya, Africa, ruining corn crops, and spreading diseases such as malaria.

Heavy snow
During El Niño, the change in Pacific Ocean currents affects the west coast of the US. Some areas may suffer floods; others become colder, seen in the high snow levels in the southern California mountains in 1998.

Seabed skeletons

Bleached coral indicates the presence of El Niño. Tiny algae live on coral and are vital to its survival. They move away when the ocean's temperature rises, leaving behind the coral's white "skeleton." With higher temperatures, coral reefs become barren and die.

Drought alert

El Niño reduces rainfall in Brazil, which can lead to drought. During the 1987 El Niño, Brazil's grain production fell by 80 percent. In 1992, scientists were able to predict El Niño, and so farmers planted crops that would survive a drought.

Burning up

In 1998, El Niño brought drought to Sumatra, Indonesia. It dried the trees and forest fires burned for weeks, covering Sumatra with thick smoke. It was so dark that drivers used headlights during the day.

All dried up

During an El Niño, winds push warm water east toward South America and away from Australia in the west. The cooler waters around eastern Australia lead to reduced rainfall, and large areas suffer from drought, causing many farmers to abandon their land.

Washed away

Much of the west coast of South America is very dry because its coastal waters are normally cool. During the 1998 El Niño, however, rain began to fall at an incredible rate. Floods broke riverbanks and swept away villages.

Freaky conditions

Earth's atmosphere and the Sun provide all of the Earth's weather conditions. Most people experience sunshine, wind, rain, and perhaps snow, but the Sun and atmosphere can also create strange conditions. Many people have seen a rainbow, caused by sunlight hitting raindrops and bouncing back; few have seen a moonbow. Other tricks of light include haloes, mirages, and the spooky Brocken Specter, while electric charges are responsible for the beautiful aurora lights.

Mysterious glow
St. Elmo's Fire is a rare light that glows at the tips of pointed objects during an electric storm. The glow may be caused when the point leaks an electric charge that is attracted to the charge of a thundercloud.

A ghostly sight
Some mountain climbers see huge human figures. The figures are just the climbers' shadows cast on the bases of nearby clouds—an effect called the Brocken Specter. The shadows may have colorful haloes called Brocken Bows.

Colors in the sky
When the Sun is low behind you and it is raining, you may see a rainbow. Sunlight reflects off raindrops, bending as it travels through them. Each color that makes up sunlight bends at a different angle, and so a rainbow appears as a band of colors.

Colors at moonrise
When a bright full Moon rises in the east and the Sun sets in the west, you may see a rare moonbow. This forms in the same way as a rainbow, so the Moon must be behind you and it must be raining in the west.

More snow gathers on the outside as the hollow cylinder of snow moves

Glowing globes
People worldwide have reported balls of light that hover in midair or drift along before exploding or fading away. This ball lightning is likely electrical, caused by thunderstorms.

Magical snowballs
When new snow falls on old and is blown by a strong warm wind, snow sometimes rolls itself up. It is rare to see them forming, but you may find a whole field full of spontaneous snowballs.

Rock reflected in the sand gives the illusion of water

Distorted view
Mirages are produced when light from distant objects bends as it passes through air at different temperatures, causing people to think they see shimmering, watery reflections in the desert.

Sun halo
When sunlight passes through cirrus (high-altitude) clouds, a halo can be seen around the Sun. Folklore says that haloes are a sign of imminent rain, which has some truth to it; cirrus clouds do often precede rainfall.

Auroras
These displays of colored light can often be seen near the North and South poles. The light is produced high in the atmosphere as electrically charged solar particles are attracted toward the magnetic poles and collide with air molecules.

Sunset spark
On a clear day, as the Sun sets or rises, a green flash may light the sky. It is visible only over a definite horizon and is caused by sunlight being bent and scattered by dust particles in the atmosphere.

Beyond Earth

The Sun is a star orbited by eight planets and their moons. The Sun's radiation causes weather on Earth by heating the atmosphere. Mercury and many moons have no atmosphere, and so no wind, rain, or snow. Venus and Mars do have atmospheres; some of their weather is similar to Earth's. The gases of Jupiter, Saturn, Uranus, and Neptune swirl around as the planets spin, forming spiral storms similar to hurricanes. Farther from the Sun, dwarf planets are far too cold for an atmosphere to form.

Blue Neptune
Neptune's 1,500-mph (2,500-kph) winds are the strongest in the solar system. Methane gas in its atmosphere cools and freezes as it rises, forming white cloud bands (above).

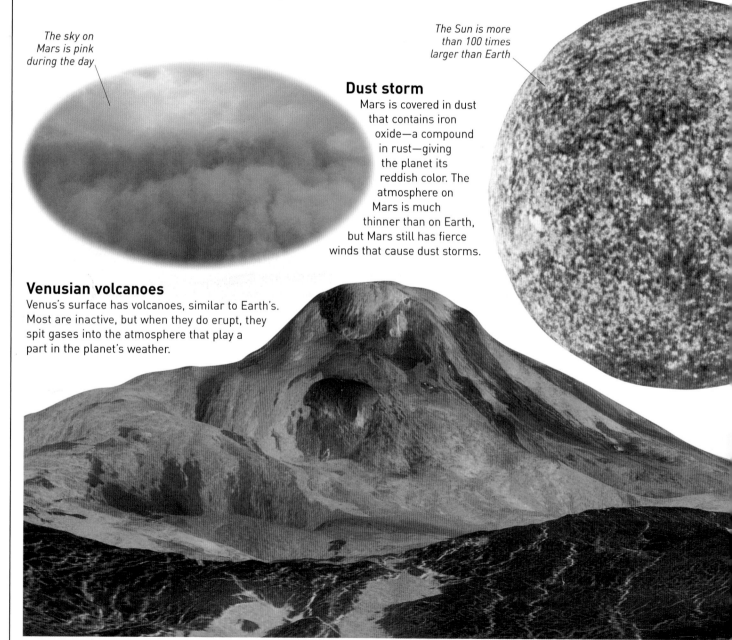

The sky on Mars is pink during the day

The Sun is more than 100 times larger than Earth

Dust storm
Mars is covered in dust that contains iron oxide—a compound in rust—giving the planet its reddish color. The atmosphere on Mars is much thinner than on Earth, but Mars still has fierce winds that cause dust storms.

Venusian volcanoes
Venus's surface has volcanoes, similar to Earth's. Most are inactive, but when they do erupt, they spit gases into the atmosphere that play a part in the planet's weather.

Stunning rings

Saturn, like all the gas giants, is nearly all atmosphere, and it becomes more dense the closer to the center you go. The planet is warmed by the Sun, but in some places the outer atmosphere is still a chilly -310°F (-190°C).

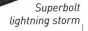
Superbolt lightning storm

High-powered winds of up to 1,100 mph (1,800 kph) encircle Saturn

Scorching storm

The Sun is a ball of extremely hot gas, increasing in heat as you head to the core. The surface is turbulent: huge storms (prominences), caused by the Sun's magnetic field, throw millions of tons of hot gas into space.

Storm prominence erupts on the Sun

Ultraviolet image of the Sun

Spinning spots

Jupiter takes less than 10 hours to make one rotation. This causes the planet's atmosphere to swirl and the Great Red Spot (above). This spot is twice the size of Earth. It is a storm similar to a hurricane that has been raging for at least 330 years.

Charged up

Lightning on Earth is caused by updrafts of air in huge thunderclouds. Other planets have lightning, too. Jupiter has energetic lightning storms at its magnetic poles, which are partly caused by the planet's strong magnetic field.

Sulfuric cloud bands

Europa's icy surface

Icy Europa

One of Jupiter's moons, Europa, has a thin atmosphere made up largely of oxygen. This rocky ball is coated in smooth water ice. Some space scientists think liquid water might be beneath the ice, which means life could exist in Europa's seas.

Molten Venus

Venus is the hottest planet, shrouded in thick clouds of sulfuric acid. The atmospheric pressure at its surface is 90 times higher than that on Earth.

Did you know?

AMAZING FACTS

- Greenlanders have about 50 words for all their snow, such as "nittaalaq" (air thick with snow).

- There are more than eight million flashes of lightning every day.

- Cumulonimbus clouds can be 7 miles (11 km) tall.

The air rises quickly through the tall cloud

A cumulonimbus cloud

- 24 in (60 cm) of dry snow takes up the same space as 1 in (2.5 cm) of rain.

- On August 14, 1979, a rainbow was visible in North Wales for three hours.

- Thunder can be heard 6 miles (10 km) away from a storm, but lightning can be seen 60 miles (100 km) away.

- A temperature of 40°F (4°C) can feel like -14°F (-10°C) if there is a 45 mph (72 kph) wind blowing. This is known as the wind-chill factor.

- In storms, objects and animals can be picked up and dropped down again some distance away.

- More than 100 tornadoes have hit Oklahoma City—more than any other city. Texas has more tornadoes a year—125—than any other US state.

- "Male" hurricanes have caused four times more damage than "female" ones since 1979, when male/female names started being used.

On July 7, 1841, hundreds of small fish and frogs fell with rain and hail on Derby, England

- Cheyenne, Wyoming is the US hail capital. A storm in August 1985 left 6-ft- (1.8-m-) high "haildrifts."

- Permanent snow and ice cover about 12 percent of Earth's land.

- A lightning flash moves from the ground to the cloud at 23,000 miles/second (37,000 km/second).

- Hail falls on Keriche, Kenya, 132 days a year—more than on any other place on Earth.

- Park ranger Roy Sullivan suffered seven lightning strikes in 41 years. His hair was set on fire, he had chest injuries, and he was knocked out.

A tornado funnel sweeps across the ground

Fork lightning

- Lightning can travel more than 6 miles (10 km) so you can suffer a strike even if there is not a storm overhead.

- Dramatic high tides result from high winds offshore and low atmospheric pressure. A 1-millibar fall in pressure causes the ocean to rise by ½ in (1 cm); a deep depression can cause a 28-in (70-cm) rise.

- A thunderstorm can drop up to 110 million gallons (500 million liters) of rain.

QUESTIONS AND ANSWERS

The aurora borealis

Q What causes the lights known as auroras?

A Solar wind is a stream of particles flowing from the Sun's polar regions. The Earth's magnetic shield protects us from this wind, but at the poles the particles create light displays as they collide with molecules in the upper atmosphere. Near the North Pole the lights are known as the aurora borealis; near the South Pole, the aurora australis.

Q What is the blanket effect?

A At night, clouds reduce the heat that leaves Earth, keeping Earth warm. This is the blanket effect.

Q What can happen where oceans meet?

A Where oceans meet, such as off the tips of South America and South Africa, storms create huge waves. At Cape Horn, they can be 65 ft (20 m) tall.

Q What are the doldrums?

A The doldrums are a windless area of rising hot air around the equator. The rising air forms cumulonimbus clouds that produce thunderstorms and waterspouts.

Record Breakers

- In April 2011, the worst tornado outbreak in the world saw 358 tornadoes hit 21 US states in four days. Thousands were injured and 348 died.

- The lowest recorded temperature in the world is -129°F (-89.2°C), taken at Vostok, Antarctica, on July 21, 1983.

- The wettest place on Earth, with an annual rainfall of 472 in (12,000 mm) is Mawsynram, Meghalaya State, India.

- The wettest day in the world was at Foc-Foc, Ile de Reunio, Indian Ocean, where 71 in (1,825 mm) of rain fell in 24 hours.

- The windiest place in the world is Port Martin, Antarctica, where winds can average more than 40 mph (64 kph) on at least 100 days each year.

- The greatest snowfall recorded in one day was at Silver Lake, Colorado on April 14, 1921, with a fall of 6 ft 3 in (1.93 m).

Ice crystals in a snowflake

A surfer enjoys South Africa's big waves

Timeline

Hurricanes, tornadoes, and other extreme weather have caused terrible suffering over the years. This timeline charts some of the worst events over the past five centuries. Although we are now more knowledgeable about the causes of extreme weather and can better predict it, we cannot avoid the terrible destruction it brings.

Flooding on the plains of India

A ship from the Spanish Armada

• **1495** A hurricane strikes Christopher Columbus near Hispaniola.

• **1559** A hurricane sinks almost all 74 Spanish ships heading to retake Florida.

• **1588** A violent May storm in the Bay of Biscay scatters the Spanish Armada ships on their way to invade England. The ships set off again in July.

• **1635** The Great Colonial Hurricane hits New England in August, causing a 20-ft (6-m) tide in Boston, which destroys thousands of trees and homes.

• **1697** Lightning strikes an Irish castle, setting fire to its gunpowder store and causing the castle to explode.

• **1780** The Great Hurricane kills 22,000 (more than any other) in the Caribbean and destroys British and French fleets.

• **1843** A brutal hailstorm destroys crops and greenhouses in Norfolk, England.

• **1876–79** A prolonged, severe drought in northern China kills between nine and 13 million people.

• **1887** The Yellow River floods 10,000 sq miles (26,000 sq km) in China; 900,000–2.5 million people die.

• **1888** A hailstorm of baseball-sized hailstones strikes Moradabad, northern India, killing 246 people.

• **1900** In September, 8–15-ft (2.4–4.5-m) storm tides inundate Galveston Island, Texas, killing 6,000.

• **1925** The Tri-State tornado causes an estimated 695 deaths in Missouri, Illinois, and Indiana.

• **1928** The San Felipe hurricane kills 3,411 in the Caribbean and Florida.

• **1930s** In the North American Midwest a drought turns farmland into a "Dust Bowl." Thousands die from heatstroke or breathing issues in the dust storms.

• **1930** A September hurricane kills thousands in the Dominican Republic and destroys its capital, Santa Domingo.

• **1931** The Yangtze River floods in China, ruining crops. About 3.7 million people perish in the floods and famine.

A storm surge rushes ashore

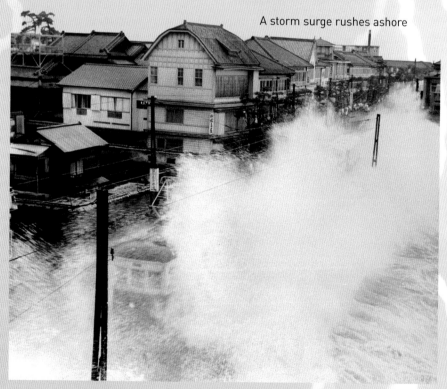

- **1953** A January storm surge of 8 ft (2.5 m) in Essex, England, kills 300; a 13 ft (4 m) surge in Holland kills 1,800.

- **1959** A hailstorm hits Selden, Kansas, on June 3, burying an area 9 miles by 6 miles (15 km by 10 km) in hailstones to a depth of 18 in (46 cm).

- **1962** A massive avalanche and mudslide in Peru kill about 4,000.

- **1963** Hurricane Flora kills more than 7,000 in Haiti and Cuba.

- **1970** A storm surge floods the Ganges Delta, killing more than 400,000.

- **1982** Monsoon floods in Orissa, India, kill 1,000 and make more than five million homeless.

- **1984** A summer hailstorm bombards Munich, Germany, with giant hailstones, causing $1 billion worth of damage.

- **1985** A million people are evacuated due to Hurricane Elena's erratic path across the Gulf of Mexico.

- **1988** Monsoon rains flood three-quarters of Bangladesh, killing 2,000 and making 30 million homeless.

A giant hailstone

- **1998** At least 2,500 people perish in an Indian heat wave in May and June.

- **1998** The Yangtze River, China, floods, killing 3,500.

- **1998** At least 2,500 die in July when a tsunami strikes Papua New Guinea.

- **1998** Two-month floods along the Nile River in Sudan make around 200,000 homeless.

- **1998** Hurricane Mitch strikes Central America in October; more than 11,000 die and 1.5 million are made homeless.

- **1999** Floods and mudslides in December kill 10,000 in Venezuela.

- **2000** Torrential February rains in Mozambique cause the worst floods for 50 years. On February 22, Cyclone Eline hits, making it even worse.

- **2003** Europe has the hottest summer for nearly 500 years. More than 20,000 deaths are blamed on the heat wave.

- **2005** Hurricane Katrina devastates the Bahamas, Florida, and New Orleans. Property damage totaled $81 billion, making it the most costly hurricane ever.

- **2013** Typhoon Haiyan crosses into the Philippines, causing mass flooding and landslides. About 13 million people are affected and at least a million houses are either totally destroyed or damaged.

The result of mudslides in Venezuela

- **1971** Hurricane Ginger wanders the North Atlantic, the Bermuda Triangle, and the coasts of North Carolina and Virginia for a record 31 days.

- **1974** On Christmas Day, Cyclone Tracy strikes Darwin, Australia, killing 50.

- **1974** Hurricane Fifi kills 10,000 in Honduras and destroys 80 percent of the banana crop.

- **1977** A tropical cyclone and storm surge strike Andhra Pradesh, India, killing 20,000 and making two million homeless.

- **1979** The 1,380-mile- (2,220-km-) wide Super Typhoon Tip is the largest recorded.

- **1980** A heat wave in the US starts forest fires; 1,000 people perish.

- **1992** Hurricane Andrew strikes the Bahamas, Florida, and Louisiana, killing 65, destroying 25,000 homes, and causing damages of $20 billion.

- **1996** A tornado takes just 30 minutes to destroy 80 villages in Bangladesh, killing more than 440 people and injuring more than 32,000.

- **1997** Lightning kills 19 people in Andhra Pradesh, India, on September 11.

- **1998** In May, a black tide of mud sweeps into Sarno, Italy, killing 130; 2,000 are made homeless.

Hurricane Elena

Find out more

There are many ways to find out more about the weather. Make or buy simple weather instruments to keep a log of hurricanes and tornadoes. You could look into projects that help victims of extreme weather, or visit a wind farm to see how people harness the weather's energy.

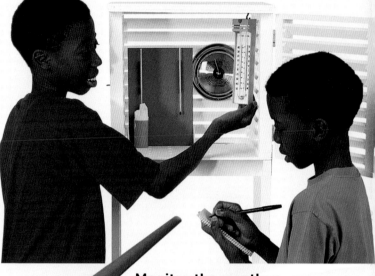

Visit a wind farm
Wind farms use wind power to generate electricity. Visit a wind farm and discover the advantages of this renewable energy resource. Find out where it is best to position the farms.

Generator converts the movement of the shaft into electricity

The blade turns to face the wind

USEFUL WEBSITES

- The National Weather Service site is an excellent starting point for learning more about storms: **www.weather.gov**
- For weather forecasts anywhere in the world go to: **weather.yahoo.com**
- To find out about people who follow hurricanes, see: **www.hurricanehunters.com**
- For information on tornadoes, visit: **www.stormtrack.org**
- For severe storm information, see: **www.nssl.noaa.gov**

Monitor the weather
Build or buy a weather center. Keep a daily log of weather measurements, such as air pressure, temperature, rainfall, and wind speed. Your class could join Student Activities in Meteorology, an online project run by the National Oceanic and Atmospheric Administration and find out about your weather and worldwide weather-related phenomena such as the greenhouse effect.

Hurricane crasher!
Find out how teams in the US and Australia track hurricanes to learn more about them in trucks and planes. They take photographs and measurements, and the planes fly right into the eye of hurricanes.

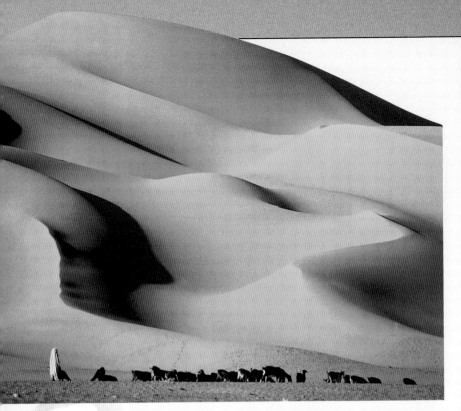

Stop the desert

Discover how people, animals, and plants survive with little rainfall. In northern Africa, drought, overgrazing, and removal of trees for firewood are resulting in the expansion of the Sahara Desert. Learn about the grass-planting projects to stop the desert spreading.

Flood benefits

Floods can cause damage, but they can sometimes be beneficial. They can increase soil fertility or create an environment for wildlife. The Ouse Washes, Cambridgeshire, UK, flood every winter, attracting thousands of migrating birds.

About 7,000 migrating swans gather on the Ouse Washes each winter

Flood warnings

Contact the National Weather Service for flood alerts. Check the Interactive Weather Information Network (IWIN) page at iwin.nws.noaa.gov/iwin. See if you can visit floodgates, such as the Glen Canyon Dam in the Colorado River or the floodgates in New Orleans.

Places to visit

THE FRANKLIN INSTITUTE SCIENCE MUSEUM WEATHER CENTER PHILADELPHIA, PENNSYLVANIA

- The center provides information on how we use science to track weather. An interactive exhibit lets visitors take part in forecasting weather. See satellite and Doppler radar images and learn about the atmospheric conditions that cause our weather.

THE GLEN CANYON DAM, ARIZONA

- The Glen Canyon Dam is part of a series of dams and reservoirs on the Colorado River that provide flood control, electricity, and water to millions. Built in the 1960s, the dam stands 710 feet (216 m) from bedrock and holds back 27 million acre-feet of water when Lake Powell is full.

EVERGLADES NATIONAL PARK, FLORIDA

- The only subtropical preserve in North America, this park is a wetland of international importance. Thousands of migrating birds winter here. The park is known for its large wading birds, such as the wood stork, great blue heron, and egrets. It is also the only place on Earth where alligators and crocodiles coexist.

THE HOOVER DAM, BOULDER CITY, NEVADA

- The dam not only provides flood control, but also stores up to two years' average flow from the Colorado River. Constructed between 1930 and 1935, the dam stands 726 feet (221 m) tall. It is part of a system that provides water to more than 18 million people in the Southwest.

Glossary

ANEMOMETER An instrument for recording wind speeds.

ATMOSPHERE The gases surrounding the Earth and some other planets.

ATMOSPHERIC PRESSURE The pressure from the atmosphere's weight.

AURORA Bands of light across the sky, visible near the North and South poles.

AVALANCHE A fall of snow and ice down a mountain.

BAROCYCLONOMETER An early device used to calculate the position of an approaching cyclone. It measured atmospheric pressure and wind direction.

BAROGRAPH A chart with vertical or horizontal bars showing amounts.

BAROMETER An instrument for measuring atmospheric pressure, to determine weather changes or altitude.

BEAUFORT SCALE A wind speed scale, from 0 (calm) to 12 (hurricane force).

BLIZZARD A strong, bitterly cold wind accompanied by heavy snow.

CLIMATE The usual, long-term weather conditions of an area.

CUMULONIMBUS CLOUD A billowing, white or dark-gray cloud that is very tall. Also called a thunderhead, this type of cloud is associated with thunderstorms. The top of the cloud is often the shape of an anvil, and the bottom can be quite dark if it is full of rain or hail.

Digital anemometer

An early barometer

CYCLONE An area of low atmospheric pressure with winds spiraling in toward it—counterclockwise in the northern hemisphere, clockwise in the southern.

DEPRESSION A body of moving air that is below normal atmospheric pressure. Depressions often bring rain.

DOLDRUMS Areas near the equator with very light winds or calms.

DROUGHT A long period of little rainfall.

DUST DEVIL A strong, mini whirlwind that whips up dust and litter into the air.

EL NIÑO A warming of the eastern tropical Pacific Ocean occurring every few years and disrupting weather patterns.

FLASH FLOOD A sudden torrent, usually caused by a heavy storm.

FLOOD When water overflows, such as from a river, and covers usually dry land.

FOG A mass of water droplets hanging in the air and reducing visibility.

GLOBAL WARMING An increase in the average temperature worldwide, believed to be caused by the greenhouse effect.

GREENHOUSE EFFECT The sprocess in which gases absorb infrared radiation emitted by the Earth's surface that would otherwise escape into space.

HAILSTONE A pellet of ice falling from cumulonimbus clouds that have very strong rising air currents.

HAILSTORM A storm in which hail falls.

HUMIDITY Amount of moisture in air.

HURRICANE A severe, often destructive storm, also called a tropical cyclone; known as typhoons in the Pacific Ocean and cyclones in the Indian Ocean.

HURRICANE CHASERS People who chase after hurricanes to learn more about them.

HYGROMETER An instrument that measures moisture in the air.

ICE AGE A period of time when ice covers a large part of the Earth's land.

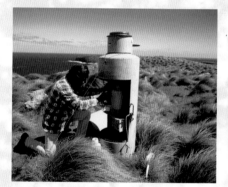
A meteorologist examines a rainfall monitor

ICE STORM When water in the air freezes and coats everything in ice.

JET STREAM A long current of air about 7.5 miles (12 km) above Earth's surface. Jet streams are hundreds of miles long, 60 miles (100 km) wide, and about half a mile (1 km) deep. They can reach speeds of 200–300 mph (300–500 kph).

LANDSLIDE The slipping of a large amount of rock and soil down the side of a mountain or cliff.

LIGHTNING A flash of light during a thunderstorm, when electricity is discharged between two clouds or between a cloud and the ground.

LIGHTNING CONDUCTOR A metal strip fixed between the highest part of a building and the ground to provide a safe route to the ground for the lightning.

METEOROLOGY The study of the Earth's atmosphere, of how weather forms, and of methods of forecasting the weather.

MONSOON A seasonal wind in south Asia. In summer it blows from the southwest and brings heavy rains; in winter it blows from the northeast.

PRECIPITATION When water vapor condenses in the atmosphere and falls to Earth as rain, snow, hail, sleet, or dew.

Under the Wave off Kanagawa by Hokusai

RAINBOW An arc of colors across the sky caused by the refraction and reflection of sunlight through the rain.

SANDSTORM A strong wind that whips up clouds of sand, especially in a desert.

SMOG A mixture of smoke and fog.

SPATE The fast flow of water in a river.

STORM SURGE A dramatic high tide that may produce flooding. Caused by the sudden pressure drop and high winds of an offshore storm.

SUPERCELL A particularly large pocket of rising air that brings massive amounts of water into a thundercloud. Supercells can generate tornadoes and waterspouts.

TEMPERATURE A measurement of how hot a body or substance is.

THERMOMETER A temperature gauge, usually with a liquid column that expands or contracts in a sealed tube.

THERMOSCOPE A device that indicates variations in temperature without measuring their amounts.

THUNDERBOLT A flash of lightning accompanied by thunder.

THUNDERCLAP A loud cracking noise caused by atmospheric gases expanding rapidly when heated suddenly by lightning.

THUNDERHEAD A towering cumulonimbus cloud that is electrically charged. A thunderhead is dark in color because it is full of rain or hail.

THUNDERSTORM A storm caused by strong rising air currents, featuring thunder, lightning, and usually heavy rain or hail.

TIDAL WAVE An unusually large wave not actually caused by the tides at all, but by an earthquake. The correct name for it is a tsunami.

TORNADO Also known as a cyclone, a whirlwind, or a twister. A tornado is a violent storm in which winds whirl around a small area of very low pressure. There is usually a dark, funnel-shaped cloud reaching down to Earth and causing damage.

TORNADO ALLEY The name given to the parts of Kansas, Missouri, and Oklahoma that are most at risk from tornadoes.

A weather satellite

TSUNAMI A huge, destructive wave caused by an earthquake on the seabed.

VORTEX A whirling mass of liquid or gas, such as tornadoes and hurricanes.

WATERSPOUT A whirling water column drawn up from the surface by a whirlwind traveling over water.

WEATHER SATELLITE A device that orbits the Earth and sends back data to help scientists forecast the weather.

WHIRLWIND A column of air whirling around an area of low pressure, and moving across the land or the surface of the ocean.

Flooding caused by monsoon rains in Vietnam

Index

Acknowledgments

Dorling Kindersley would like to thank:
Sheila Collins for design assistance.
Indexer: Helen Peters
Illustrators: Eric Thomas and John Woodcock
Photographers: Peter Anderson, Jeoff Brightling, Jane Burton, Peter Chadwick, Andy Crawford, Geoff Dann, Mike Dunning, Steve Gorton, Frank Greenaway, Ellen Howden, Colin Keates, Dave King, Andrew Nelmerm, Janet Peckham, Kim Sayer, Karl Shone, Andreas Von Einsiedel, Jerry Young, and Michel Zabé

For this edition, the publisher would also like to thank: Hazel Beynon for text editing and Carron Brown for proofreading.

The publisher would like to thank the following for their kind permission to reproduce their photographs:
(Key: t=top, b=below, l=left, r=right, c=center)

Alamy Images: Paul Wood 50–51c, Reven T. C. Wurman 22–23b; **Alison Anholt White:** 14c; **Ardea London Ltd.:** Francois Gohier 10bl; M. Watson 41bl; **Associated Press Ap:** 39tl, 43tl, 43b; SLF Jennings 30–31; Topham 52tr; **Bridgeman Art Library, London/New York:** Thor's fight with

the Giants, 1872 by Winge, Marten Eskil 1825–96, National Museum, Stockholm, Sweden; Plato and Aristotle, detail of the School of Athens, 1510–1511 (fresco), Vatican Museum and Galleries 6bc; **British Museum, London:** 7ca, 7cr; **Bruce Coleman Ltd.:** Jules Cowan; 57tr Jeff Foott 2b, 14–15; Johnny Johnson 55bc; Allan G. Potts 58–59b; **Corbis:** Aurora Open/Patrick Orton 44–45b, epa/Paris Barrera 33b, Imaginechina 44cl, NASA 32bl, NOAA/CNP 32clb, Reuters/Sue Ogrocki 22tl; **Corbis UK Ltd.:** 40r, 41r; Bettmann 7cr, 24crb, 42cl, 47c; Lowell Georgia 4tr, 40tl; David Muench 56cl; Galen Rowell 41cr; Dave Bartruff 68l; Bettmann 66br; Rick Doyle 65b; El Universal/Sygma 66cl; Chris Golley 64tr; Historical Picture Archive 71l; Aaron Horowitz 64bl; George McCarthy 69cl; Sygma 68br; A. & J. Verkaik 64–65 bckgrd; Michael S. Yamashita 71b; **Dreamstime.com:** Khunaspix 23tr, Lastdays1 23cra, 23crb, R. Gino Santa Maria 23cr, 23crb (Saint Louis), 23br; **Sylvia Cordaiy Photo Library Ltd:** Nigel Rolstone 24–25b; **Ecoscene:** Nick Hawkes 40bl; **Environmental Images:** John Arnold 49cr; **E.T. Archive:** Guildhall Library 56cr; **European Space Agency:** 71tr; **Mary Evans Picture Library:** 24bc, 28cl, 66cl; **Getty Images:** 45tl, 45tr, 45cr, AFP 45c, Boston Globe 16br; **Glasgow Museums, The Burrell Collection:** 46tl; **Ronald Grant Archive:** WB & Universal 20–21cl; **Robert Harding Picture Library:** 11cl,

11b, 36–37a; Jon Gardley 49tr; Dr. A.C. Waltham 36–37b; **Hulton Getty:** Fox 36cr; Tony Waltham 43tr; G. Williams Photos 38tr; Keystone 34cl; Painted by Stephen Pearce, engraved by John Scott 14tl; **Hutchison Library:** 35r; **ICRC:** Clive Shirley 53bl; **INAH:** Mexican Museum Authority, Michael Zabe 7bl; **Kristen Klaver:** 51clb, 51bl; **FLPA—Images of nature:** 30–31cra; J.C. Allen 26bl; D. Hoadley 20–21c; H. Hoflinger 18cr; NRC 27cl; R. Jennings 60c; S. Jonasson 13br; **Magnum:** Bruce Davidson 15ca; Steve McCurry 42bl; **Gene Moore:** 26–27, 27tl, 27cr; **N.A.S.A.:** 2tr, 2c, 4cl, 2cl, 28–29, 51br, 62tr, 62–63c, 62b, 63c, 63bl, 63br, 63r, 4bc, 16cl; Bill Hrybyk 33tc, Boeing/Carleton Bailie 51br, Robert Simmon 44tr; **National Maritime Museum, London:** 8cr; **Nature Picture Library:** Mike Lane 69cl; **Courtesy of the National Science Foundation:** 49tl, 49cla; **NHPA:** A.N.T. 19cr; **NOAA:** Dennis J. Sigrist, International Tsunami Information Centre, Honolulu, Hawaii 36b; NOAA Photo Library, NOAA Central Library; OAR/ERL/National Severe Storms Laboratory (NSSL) 23c; **Novosti:** A. Varfolomeyer 26tr; **Oxford Scientific Films:** Daniel J. Cox 48cl; Warren Faidley 4bl, 17br, 25a, 28tl; Michael Fogden 46c; Richard Henman 58bl; Mantis Wildlife Films 54cr; Colin Monteath, Hegehog House 34b; Ian West 20–21clb; Stan Osolinksi 60cl; Stouffer Enterprises Inc./Animals Animals 12b; **Panos Pictures:** Trygue Bolstad 47bl; Heidi Bradner 11tr; Jerry Callow 6cl; Neil Cooper 47cb; Jeremy Hartley 46tr, 62cl; Sim Holmes 2tc, 28bl; Zed Nelson 28tr; Clive Shirley 58c, 59bc; © Tatlow 59tr; **PA News Photo Library:** EPA/Pool 14tr; **Pitt Rivers Museum, Oxford:** 7cra; **Planet Earth Pictures:** Georgette Douwma 59tl; Jiri Lochman 59cr; **John E. Purchase:** 60bl; **Rex Features:** 14cl, 30tr, 42br, 43cl, 52bl; Jean Yves Desfoux 38cl; Sipa Press 18–19; **Courtesy Of The**

Rosenberg Library, Galveston, Texas: 30bl; **Royal British Columbia Museum:** 56bl. **Scala:** Museo della Scienza Firenze 2tl, 4br, 8br, 8l, 9bl; S. Maria Novella (farmacia), Firenze 9c; **Science Photo Library:** NASA 44cr; Eric Bernard, Jerrican 38bl; Jean–Loup Charmet 24c; Jim Goodwin 52cl; Ben Johnson 36cl; Damien Lovegrove 60crb; Pete Menzel 24cl NASA. 25bc; NASA GSFC 58tr; Claude Nuridsany & Marie Perennesu 3tl, 38cr; David Parker 50bl, 51tr, 57cl; Pekka Parviainen 61clb; Fred K. Smith 5bc, 16tr; 70–71 bckgrd; Brian Brake 66tr; Cape Grim B.A.P.S/Simon Fraser 70r; Simon Fraser 70bl; NASA 67br; NCAR 67t; Kazuyoshi Nomachi 69tl; Claude Nuridsany & Marie Perennou 65cr; Pekka Parviainen 64tl, 65tl; Victor de Schwanberg 68–69 bckgrd; **Still Pictures:** Adrian Arbib 53br; Nigel Dickenson 52br; Filho–UNEP 59c; G. Grifiths/ Christian Aid 58clb; Olivier Langrand 54cb; Andre Maslennikor 46bc; Gil Moti 34cr; Hartmut Schwarzbach 46br, 53tr; Hjalte Tin 53cl; UNEP. 61; **Courtesy of Jeff Piotrowski/ Storm Productions Inc. USA:** 4cr, 18cl, 18clb, 18bl, 20–21tr, 20–21br; **Tony Stone Images:** 56–57b; Vince Streano 31crb; **Stock Shot:** Gary Pearl 40cb; **Sygma:** 31cra, 31br; Paul/Pierre Pollin 39b; Claude Poulet 48tr; **Topham Picturepoint:** 20–21r; **Travel Ink:** David Toase 30tr; **University of Chicago:** 23tl; **Weathershot:** Warren Faidley 4tl, 5tr, 10tr, 11cr, 39tr, 50bc, 51tl, 61cl, 63cr.

All other images © Dorling Kindersley
For further information see:
www.dkimages.com